OPPORTUNITIES IN
CAD/CAM CAREERS

Jan Bone

VGM Career Horizons
a division of *NTC Publishing Group*
Lincolnwood, Illinois USA

Cover Photo Credits

Clockwise from top left: DeVry Inc; American Printer; Honeywell; ABB Robotics.

Library of Congress Cataloging-in-Publication Data

Bone, Jan.
    Opportunities in computer aided design and computer aided
manufacturing careers / Jan Bone.

        p.   cm. — (VGM opportunities series)
    ISBN 0-8442-4084-2 (hard) — ISBN 0-8442-4085-0 (soft)
    1. Computer-aided design—Vocational guidance. 2. CAD/CAM
systems—Vocational guidance.   I. Title.   II. Series.
TA174.B67   93-17885
                                                        CIP

Published by VGM Career Horizons, a division of NTC Publishing Group
4255 West Touhy Avenue
Lincolnwood (Chicago), Illinois 60646-1975, U.S.A.
© 1994 by NTC Publishing Group. All rights reserved.
No part of this book may be reproduced, stored in a retrieval system,
or transmitted in any form or by any means,
electronic, mechanical, photocopying, recording or otherwise,
without the prior permission of NTC Publishing Group.
Manufactured in the United States of America.

3 4 5 6 7 8 9 0 VP 9 8 7 6 5 4 3 2 1

CONTENTS

ABOUT THE AUTHOR

As a technical writer who has toured a number of industrial sites and laboratories, Jan Bone has had the chance to see CAD/CAM and related technologies in action. Today, if she were a young person beginning a career, she says, she'd be a manufacturing engineer. Factory automation (and CAD/CAM is an important component) offers opportunities for those who enjoy high-tech challenges.

Jan's career as a writer, however, spans nearly 50 years. Ever since her first newspaper job on the Williamsport (Pennsylvania) *Sun,* she has enjoyed the fast-moving world of deadlines and changing topics. Her writing covers a variety of subjects: from celebrity interviews to human interest features in magazines like *Family Circle* and *Woman's World,* to technical articles in professional journals like *Safety and Health* and *Hazmat World: the Magazine for Environmental Management.* Her 1989 article and photographs about the Soviet agro-industrial complex were published in U.S. and international editions of *Food Engineering.*

She wrote the chapter on Automated Processes for the National Safety Council's *Accident Prevention Manual, 10th edition,* and the "White Paper" for the National Safety Council's Ergonomics Symposium. In addition, she writes two newsletters for them: *Product Safety Up-to-Date,* and *Global Safety, Health, and Environment Update.*

Jan is an associate member of the Society of Manufacturing Engineers (SME), and of several of its divisions: Robotics International

(RI), Computer and Automated Systems Association (CASA), and Machine Vision Association (MVA). In addition, she is an associate member of the Institute of Industrial Engineers, and of the American Society for Training and Development. Jan is also a charter member of the Global Automation Information Network (GAIN), an organization dedicated to the successful use of robotics and machine vision automation.

A prolific free-lance writer, Jan is senior writer for the *Chicago Tribune's* special advertising sections. Her home computers and her laptop computer are linked by modem to the *Tribune's* mainframe, and she uses a store-forward fax service to stay in touch with editors. Through electronic database searching, she can access files from more than 90 national and international newspapers. In addition, she can view SME's upcoming events, learn about new books and videos, and chat electronically with other SME members by using SME's bulletin board.

From 1977 to 1985, Jan was an elected member of the board of trustees of William Rainey Harper College in Palatine, Illinois, and served as its secretary from 1979–85. During that time, the college set up a CAD/CAM Center (computer-aided design and computer-aided manufacturing), sparking Jan's interest in factory automation.

Since 1983, she has been listed in *Who's Who of American Women.* She has won the Chicago Working Newsman's Scholarship, the Illinois Education Association School Bell Award for Best Comprehensive Coverage of Education by dailies under 250,000 circulation, and the American Political Science Association Award for Distinguished Reporting of Public Affairs.

A graduate of Cornell University, Jan earned her M.B.A. degree at Roosevelt University. She has taught adult education classes in writing for over 20 years, and is also a lecturer in composition classes at Roosevelt University.

She is married, the mother of four married sons, and grandmother of Emily Diane and Jennifer Marie.

ACKNOWLEDGMENTS

The following individuals were especially helpful in the development of this book: Bruce Bickford, Harold Blanthorn, Rex Davenport, Juan Diaz, Pete Diepersloot, Philip Farrelly, John Hangey, Brad Holtz, Neele Johnston, Chris Kidd, Jim Lakatos, James Luxho, Dennis Mueller, Bill Omurtag, Doug Speidel, Susan Steelman, Mary Thompson, Donald A. Vincent, Currin R. Webster, Shelly Weide.

Special thanks to Carol Bartz and Christopher Kidd.

The author also wishes to thank the following organizations for their assistance: Accreditation Board for Engineering and Technology; Autodesk, Inc.; Berhan Industries, Ltd.; Hudson Control Group, Inc.; Institute of Industrial Engineers; *Minority Engineer;* National Society of Black Engineers; *P/O/P Times;* Productive Technologies; Robotic Industries of America (RIA); Seagate Technology; Society of Manufacturing Engineers (SME); Society of Women Engineers (SWE).

FOREWORD

Computer-aided design and computer-aided manufacturing (CAD/CAM) together represent one of the fastest growing sectors for career opportunities. Knowledge and training in CAD/CAM may lead you into careers in architecture, design, engineering, and manufacturing. CAD/CAM can also open the door for diverse opportunities in aerospace, marketing and communications, video graphics, robotics, and a host of technology-driven industries. *Opportunities in CAD/CAM* describes each career area in depth. It also explains the education, qualifications, and experience you need to enter into and advance in this exciting and evolving field.

The Editors of VGM

CHAPTER 1

COMPUTER-AIDED DESIGN AND COMPUTER-AIDED MANUFACTURING: IMPORTANT TECHNOLOGIES

Seat belts fastened, seats in the upright position, tray tables in place and locked, and all carry-on luggage stowed under your seat or in the overhead compartments . . . You've followed the flight attendant's instructions, and you're ready for takeoff on what may seem like a routine flight.

But if you're a passenger in the newest United Airlines jet, the Boeing 777, you and your more-than-400 fellow travelers probably haven't guessed that you're riding in the first commercial jet designed entirely on a computer system, rather than on paper!

The high-tech design/build approach that allowed Boeing to put together a plane with 85,000 major components and more than four million parts without building a full-scale production mockup—a *first* in the company's half-century history—is an offshoot of CAD/CAM.

Computer-aided design, computer-aided manufacturing, (CAD/CAM) and computer-aided engineering (CAE)—separately, or together—are technologies that offer job opportunities in an ever-increasing variety of fields.

At Boeing, for instance, nearly 4,000 engineers worked with production personnel, supplier representatives, and airline workers in 238 "design/build" teams to create the 777. The most complex commercial plane ever built, this twin-engine jet can carry more passengers farther (over 6,000 miles) than any two-engine commercial jet has previously done.

The 777 was designed in a computer system that consists of eight IBM mainframes, 2,200 workstations, and a sophisticated design application (developed by a French company) that lets design engineers create, configure, specify, and check parts at their workstations.

That's CAD.

In a different application, CAD technology allows the United Group's Craig Smith to "show" a Big Three automaker his concept for a point-of-purchase advertising display for a new-car showroom. Up front.

"I can do a 3-dimensional computer drawing of the project and make it photo-realistic," Smith explains. "On the computer, I can show the client how the light in the showroom will interact with the materials we'll use to build the display, whether they're woodgrain or shiny metal. I can take a photo of an actual showroom, including people, and scan that photo into the computer, merging it with the computer drawings of the display."

In short, before Smith's company ever builds the project, the P-O-P designer and the auto company have agreed on what the display will look like in its final end-user environment. CAD has made it possible for them to "see."

Architectural firms like Houston's Archimage say CAD and computers represent a fundamental change in the way architects do their work. To get clients actively involved in the design process, the company makes presentations on a 37-inch monitor, so everyone is directly involved in making decisions. Realistic two- and three-dimensional animation and multimedia production techniques made possible by integrating CAD with computer animation add life to the company presentations.

"Clients can instantly 'see' on a computer the results of changes in lighting or materials," says Archimage founder and president Richard Buday. "They can get the feel of what a building will look like if it is constructed with glass versus brick." Once the firm has completed the design, the architect can take clients on an animated fly-over and walk-through of the entire building, allowing them to explore every element of the design. On the computer screen, they can even open doors and walk through rooms!

CAD—combined with CAM—speeds turnaround time for designers who make presentations to clients. For instance, designers can send CAD files via modem or disk to Envison Design Centers in San Francisco, Los Angeles, and New York. After the files have been received, they're transferred to LaserCAMM, a high-speed, computer-controlled laser cutter, that cuts up to 1/4-inch thick material from any CAD drawing in a DXF format. The system creates high-quality 3D models, prototypes, or visual aids from plastics, wood, matte board, or fabrics. The Design Centers cut the parts within 24 hours and ship the parts back to the client by overnight air.

Today's modern CAD/CAM systems—especially if they're integrated with management and office functions—store an incredible amount of information. Ingersoll Milling Machine Company, a medium-sized manufacturer of low-cost machine tools for the global market, has a computer-integrated enterprise covering a variety of functions: proposals, comprehensive customer master file, order receipt, engineering design, release to manufacturing, procurement of materials, parts machining, subassembly, final assembly, test, field installation, cost tracking, purchasing, inventory, accounts receivable, CAD, CAM, and comprehensive management reporting for all of these functions.

The company has 287 graphics (CADAM) mainframe workstations, and 600 alphanumeric (CICS) workstations. Its computer operators access the 68 *billion* character integrated database on an average of 9 million times on the first work shift every day! The company runs the system on a central processor with 256 megabytes of main memory and a processing rate of 72 million instructions per second.

ADVENT OF CAD/CAM

Four decades ago, the computer field was dominated by large, centralized computing systems. To a certain extent, especially in large companies like Ingersoll, those systems still play a major role. Today, though, at the other end of the spectrum are smaller (but interconnected) personalized systems—a market driven by innovations that brought the personal computer within technological and financial reach of millions.

Computer developments have also changed the manufacturing scene. In today's highly competitive manufacturing environment, increasing numbers of organizations are considering installing automation or expanding its use. Whether a company chooses to set up islands of automation or to operate a dedicated, hard automated assembly line with virtually no human intervention, one thing is certain. Advances in technology—led by the rapid pace of developments in computers—are changing the demand for workers who develop, maintain, and use that technology.

In the late 1950s, manufacturers began to move towards automation by installing numerical control on machine tools. In the mid-1970s, companies like Ingersoll began to install NC machining centers as islands of automation. And in the future, says Ingersoll's George J. Hess, "We're shifting our focus to the effective use of knowledge, the acquisition of knowing, the recording and classification of knowledge, and to the disbursement of it to critical points throughout the entire enterprise. The next step will be a whole new class of strategically important systems that we are unable to handle with today's procedural deterministic programming methods."

Hess brings up an important point when he talks about *the next step.* Today's successful companies are planning ahead . . . working towards time-based competitiveness. In the manufacturing sphere, that means shortening the time required for product and process design engineering and reducing time-to-market through automation.

Given today's global environment, automation can be the key to survival. To be effective, however, automation must be programmable—that is, automation must be flexible enough to perform a variety of tasks. Computer technology and communications technology make this possible.

FIVE MAJOR TECHNOLOGIES

Five major technologies are involved in programmable automation. They are:

Computer-Aided Design (CAD). Simple forms of CAD are used as an electronic drawing board, often by drafters and design engineers. CAD can also help a designer or engineer make changes in an existing product. In more complex and sophisticated installations, CAD is combined with computer-aided engineering (CAE) to help engineers analyze and improve designs, through modeling and simulation, before products are actually built.

Versions of simulation software, such as Centric Engineering System's Spectrum, can solve problems involving multiple types of physics. It's used for tough problems ranging from design of airbags to simulating metal forming processes.

Numerically Controlled (NC) Tools. NC machine tools are devices that follow programmed instructions to cut or form a piece of metal. The instructions tell the machine the desired dimensions and the steps for the process. The term CNC refers to computer-numerically controlled machine tools.

Flexible Manufacturing Systems (FMS). A computer-integrated group of clusters of multiple NC machines or workstations. They are linked together with work-transfer devices, for the complete automatic processing of different product parts, or the assembly of parts into differing units.

Industrial Robots. An industrial robot is basically a manipulator which can be programmed to move objects.

Many countries and users have accepted the definition of the Robotic Industries Association (RIA), a U.S.-based trade association of companies that use or are considering using robotic equipment, as well as companies that manufacture or market robotic equipment. RIA defines robot as "a reprogrammable, multifunctional manipulator designed to move materials, parts, tools or other specialized devices, through variable programmed motions for the performance of a variety of tasks."

Robot technology ranges from simple pick-and-place robots to intelligent robots which can decide actions by means of their sensing function and their recognizing function.

In today's industrial world, robots with grippers perform tasks in such fields as die casting, loading presses, forging and heat treating, and plastic molding. They load and unload other machines. A different kind of robot—one that can handle a tool instead of grippers, or uses its grippers to grasp a special tool—is used in applications like paint spraying; spot or arc welding; grinding, drilling, and riveting in machining.

At Lockheed's giant Sunnyvale, California, plant, robots are used in assembling printed circuit boards. In Japan, robots put tiny screws in watches, tightening them automatically in place. From aerospace plants to automotive assembly lines to appliance manufacturing, robots are helping industry increase production rates while keeping quality control constant.

Robotic Industries Association (RIA), the North American trade group that focuses exclusively on the robotics industry, estimated that in 1993, some 47,000 industrial robots were in use in the United States. Roughly half were being used in the automotive industry. Other leading user industries included appliances, electronics, food and beverage manufacturing, pharmaceuticals, and heavy equipment.

Computer-Integrated Manufacturing (CIM). In computer-integrated manufacturing, programmable automated tools are used for design, manufacturing, and management in an integrated system, with maximum coordination and communication between them. Computer-aided manufacturing (CAM) is just one part of an integrated system; it is with CIM that the most dramatic gains in productivity and cost-savings are being made.

THE CAD/CAM/CAE INDUSTRY

What do experts think about the future of technologies like CAD and CAM? More to the point, what industries are using them, and how are those industries doing? Answers to those questions will affect your chances of getting a job.

One way to keep up with business forecasts for selected industries is to read the *U.S. Industrial Outlook,* a comprehensive, easy-to-use reference book that gives you an overall picture of more than 300 industries. Issued every two years, this reference tool is sold through the U.S. Government Printing Office, Superintendent of Documents, Mail Stop: SSOP, Washington, DC 20402-9328. The book describes domestic and international markets, and forecasts growth for the year of publication, as well as for the long term. Tables and charts illustrate industry revenues, employment, production, market share, and trade patterns.

Four major sectors make up the computer-aided design, computer-aided manufacturing, and computer-aided engineering industry. They are:

Mechanical CAD/CAM/CAE—Involving tools used to design, analyze, document, and manufacture discrete parts, components, and assemblies.

Electronic Design Automation—Involving tools used to automate the design process of a variety of electronic products.

Geographic Information Systems (GIS)—In which users capture, edit, display and analyze geographically referenced data.

Architectural, Construction, and Engineering—Computer-aided software used by architects, contractors, and plant and civil engineers to aid in designing and managing buildings and industrial plants.

Using information from Dataquest, a market research firm that tracks the CAD/CAM/CAE industry, the 1993 *U.S. Industrial Outlook* forecasts the 1996 world market for hardware, software, and services at $21.05 billion . . . up from $15.3 billion in 1992.

In 1992, the CAD/CAM/CAE market for North America ($5.14 billion) represented just over one-third of the world's total. Europe (at $5.68 billion) was 37 percent; Asia (at $4.1 billion) was 26 percent; and the rest of the world was $343 million.

The 1992 figures showed a slight growth in mechanical CAD/CAM/CAE software (compared with 1991 revenues). Many engineers, designers, and architectural drafting personnel use this software; it's important in the design, engineering, and manufacturing of aircraft, automobiles, and consumer goods. World revenues from this software are expected to reach $2.57 billion by 1996—a 5.2 percent growth from 1992.

Electronic design automation (EDA) has several segments: electronic computer-aided engineering, integrated circuit layout, and printed circuit board multichip module. Although the market for electronic design automation (EDA) fell 7 percent in 1992, compared to 1991's figures, sales of software for floor-planning, and automatic placement and routing systems are projected to grow. By 1996, Dataquest predicts worldwide revenue for EDA software at $1.8 billion, up nearly 10 percent over 1992.

GIS/Mapping software (which often uses CAD technology for basic drawing), combines graphics, computer images, and database management software to map or analyze geographic and demographic information. A GIS program usually contains a series of digitized maps based on a database of data and measurements, information about relationships among the data, and a database of alphanumeric (letters and numbers) data that describe features of map areas, lines, or points. Although the U.S. government is the single largest user of the technology, gas, water, and electric utilities, and the petroleum industry, also rely on these programs. This portion of the CAD/CAM/CAE software market is projected to reach $1.3 billion in 1996—*a 20 percent growth over 1992 revenues.*

Architectural, engineering, and construction software (AEC) will also have significant growth, according to Dataquest predictions. Worldwide revenues for this market segment should reach $1.2 billion in 1996, up 14.5 percent over 1992. In 1992, however, AEC software was the fastest-growing area of the CAD/CAM/CAE industry. Increasingly, the U.S. government is demanding that small commercial developers provide it with electronic design data for government-contracted building projects.

CAD/CAM'S FUTURE

While no single source can accurately predict economic activity, you can use the *U.S. Industrial Outlook* to see how experts view the future.

If, for instance, you're thinking of working in CAD/CAM in aerospace, you'll learn that the aerospace industry is expected to decline as a result of the downturn in defense spending. If you're looking at CAD/CAM in the automotive industry, you'll find that the General Motors, Ford, and Chrysler have together established a research and development consortium: the CAD/CAM Partnership. The Partnership is developing generic technology to help bring vehicles to market sooner.

If you're considering CAD/CAM in the printed circuit board industry, you'll learn that in 1991, there were 70,000 jobs with PCB producers and 80,000 jobs with electronic contract assembly firms—many of which provide design services that traditionally use CAD technology. In addition, there are hundreds of thousands of jobs generated by the related material supplier industries and the original equipment manufacturers (OEMs) who make or assemble their own printed circuit boards. PCBs (with mounted components) are a basic building block for computers, consumer electronics, automobile controls, and industrial and military electronic systems. And in 1992, 70 percent of the boards assembled in the United States were produced with automated equipment. Automation will play an even greater role in PCB manufacturing in the future, as companies attempt to cut down their labor costs to stay competitive with offshore producers.

CAD is an essential part of a new technology—Rapid Prototyping & Manufacturing—that's helping industries increase competitiveness because it saves costs and time. RP&M is a vehicle for turning basic research and design work into finished products faster, with higher quality, and at lower cost. The geometric descriptions required for current RP&M equipment are provided by CAD systems, primarily using CAD software that can create closed models quickly and easily.

SCOPE OF THIS BOOK

Because the technology involved with programmable automation is so complex, and changing so rapidly, this book will deal with opportunities in just two main areas: Computer-Aided Design (CAD) and Computer-Aided Manufacturing (CAM) and will touch briefly on robotics. *Opportunities in Robotics Careers* (2nd ed., 1993), another book by the same author in VGM's Career Horizon series, covers robotics in more detail.

Within the limits of either book, it's impossible to cover the field comprehensively. Instead, material about the technologies, stories of people who are currently working in the fields, and information on schools and training, associations, and periodicals will help you learn where to find out what you need to know.

Do *you* want a job in computer-aided design or computer-aided manufacturing? Can you get one?

These are the questions that this edition of *Opportunities in CAD/CAM* tackles. There are no easy answers in today's job market. The global marketplace, the downturn in defense spending, and the economics of the worldwide recession of the 1990s all play a part in *your* job chances. This book, however, will give you information about various components of the CAD/CAM industry. It will give you places to go for more details, tell you how to find and use sources, and (through personal vignettes) let you know how a few people in the industry view their jobs.

One thing is certain—CAD/CAM is exciting! That's what industry veterans say. Both Chris Kidd (who used CAD technology to design cosmetics displays for Procter & Gamble Noxell's Division and a merchandising system for Kiwi shoe products), and Peter Ruszel (who uses CAD-created drawings in his shop for production purposes, interfacing his CAD system with a numerically controlled router) feel computer-aided design and manufacturing are special.

These technologies have their own special character, values, and opportunities for those who work in the industry and love it.

Maybe CAD/CAM will be special for you, too.

CHAPTER 2

HOW COMPUTER-AIDED DESIGN WORKS

The computer equipment and software sectors span seven specific industries. Computer equipment industries are electronic computers (SIC 3571), computer storage devices (SIC 3572), computer terminals (SIC 3575), and computer peripheral equipment not classified elsewhere (SIC 3577). In computer software, industries are computer programming services (SIC 7371), prepackaged software (SIC 7372), and computer integrated services design.

The U.S. government says CAD/CAM/CAE is one of the most dynamic segments of the overall computer equipment. But CAD itself isn't new. In fact, it's been around for over 30 years. In the late 1950s and early 1960s, researchers working on interactive computer graphics began to use computer screens to display and manipulate lines and shapes instead of numbers and text. By 1963, the Department of Defense had funded a project, SKETCHPAD, in which users at the Massachusetts Institute of Technology could draw pictures on a screen and manipulate them with a "light pen"—an object shaped like a pen that was wired to the computer, and located points on the screen.

(Interestingly, pen-based personal computers, introduced to the market in 1989, reached a $100 million market by 1991, with over 100 U.S. companies developing software and hardware for pen-based systems. Pen-based technology is becoming integrated into laptops, notebooks, and personal digital devices. Today, all these systems use a graphical user interface—symbols that identify keyboard functions.)

An early form of CAD was used by the Army Map Service in the mid-1960s. Original plots were made on huge tables (4 feet by 8 feet), by moving a "light pen" over a photosensitive film. Later, plots were made by scratching an emulsion off a clear film. By these means (using a variable aperture light source or styli of various widths), images could be produced in varying line widths with great accuracy. Plotters consisted of a large table with a track and moving head, rather like a track-type manual drafting machine. "Number crunching" was done on mainframe computers.

HOW CAD DEVELOPED

Early CAD systems like SKETCHPAD and the others which followed needed the power of mainframe computers—expensive units that might, at the time, cost up to a million dollars. Because of the expense and the necessity to invest in a large mainframe computer, most of the first major CAD users were manufacturers in such fields as aerospace, automobiles, and electronics. They say the benefits of CAD use were in increased productivity and better design, and they had the capital to make the necessary investment. In addition, their needs were extensive enough to justify the cost economically.

During the 1960s and 1970s, the cost of computer power decreased, as electronics manufacturers developed the ability to put more circuitry into an integrated circuit chip. Mini- and microcomputers began to be developed, and display screens became cheaper. Consequently, CAD became more popular—even commonplace—for product design, drafting, and related engineering analysis. Architects were among CAD's early users. "That's not surprising," says designer Chris Kidd. "Large buildings are basically a stack of more or less identical floorplans, with details expressed in well-established graphic symbols."

CAD FOR PERSONAL COMPUTERS

In the early 1980s, taking advantage of the phenomenal rise in popularity of the personal computer, CAD systems began to be developed that could run on desktop computers, while still connecting to other systems. No book on CAD would be complete without mentioning AutoCAD, the software program that's virtually become the international standard for computer-aided drafting and design.

The company was founded in 1982 by 13 systems programmers with a collective capital of $59,000. Combined with the phenomenal growth in popularity of the personal computer, AutoCAD brought computer-aided drafting and design within the financial reach of many smaller businesses.

Today, with more than 788,000 installed users worldwide, Autodesk reports that production drafters and professional designers use the software for a variety of applications. Autodesk, the company that developed AutoCAD, also markets and supports additional products for use on desktop computers and workstations . . . including AutoSketch, a precision drawing program; Generic CADD, a popular program in low-cost 2D drafting and design; and Autodesk 3D Studio, an award-winning 3D modeling, rendering, and animation product for video production, AutoCAD presentation, and animation.

Autodesk products are available in 17 languages, and are sold through a network of authorized dealers and distributors in 80 countries. Customer support is provided through more than 500 authorized training center locations, the Autodesk Forum on CompuServe (a major electronic bulletin board), numerous AutoCAD user groups, and more than 1,000 books, tutorials, and periodicals. In 1991, Release 11 was called "Editor's Choice" by *PC Magazine* and "Product of the Year" by *InfoWorld Magazine*). Autodesk's sales in fiscal year 1992 were over $284 million.

HOW CAD WORKS

The key to CAD is computer graphics—the use of the computer to display graphic images. The images are based on mathematical coordinates, which are just like points drawn on a graph for a geometry class. This descriptive information exists in the computer as digital electronic data. The computer makes it possible to store, retrieve, transmit, and process this data quickly and accurately, and the monitor, or display screen, shows the data as drawings.

"In the CAD world, we take a pencil out of the hand of the operator and place it into the hand of the computer," explains Marmon Pine, president of CAD Design Systems, Inc. "We do exactly the same things designers and drafting people have always done with a pencil and paper. But now we communicate with the computer, so that the messages we used to send to our fingers to direct the pencil are now sent in computer language."

At the heart of every CAD system is a computer, which works with the data the CAD operator supplies. There are several methods for giving data to the computer. One technique uses a mouse—a small, hand-held device that's moved either mechanically or optically across an array of lines on a small pad. As the mouse "runs" across the lines, it counts them, sending information to the computer about how fast it is moving and how many times it has moved. The computer uses this information to move an indicator (typically a cursor, cross-hair, or indicator circle) around the screen.

Another type of input device is called a digitizing tablet, or a stylus and tablet. The stylus is a pencil-like device that the CAD operator moves around on a tablet. The tablet varies in size; typically it is 11 inches × 11 inches, but can be as large as 4 to 5 feet wide. The position of the stylus is electronically detected and sent to the computer. Like the information sent by the mouse, the information sent by the stylus is used to move the cursor, cross-hair or indicator circle around on the screen. Technically, however, because a mouse is an incremental device, it does not digitize.

Scanners (another type of input device) can be used to trace graphic media such as drawings, maps, or photographs, and convert them into x-y point data. Scanner use is restricted in engineering CAD, however, because data are raster information . . . as Kidd says, "a picture without thought." Still, they're useful for recording existing drawings or symbol libraries.

Of course the CAD operator can type on a keyboard, sending information about the coordinates and typing in commands, just as he or she would type a letter.

It's also possible to send information from another computer to the computer the CAD operator is working on, connecting the computers directly. When a design and construction team planned the 4.2 million square foot Mall of America in the Twin Cities of Minneapolis and St. Paul, 80 people used AutoCAD on a network of personal computers to create the design and building specifications, to manage the development process, and to maintain fast, efficient communications. The project leader estimates the software's management capabilities saved an entire year of design and construction time.

Another way of transferring CAD information between computers is by using a modem—a device which lets computer equipment talk to other equipment through phone lines or computer cables. Such information is "read" by the CAD operator's computer just as if the operator had entered it on the computer, using a mouse, stylus/digitizing pad, or other input device.

Small-scale CAD users may not possess a modem compatible with those used by larger firms. Or the two computers may be too far apart to run cable between them. Consequently, information is often transferred between two computers by having the operator saving CAD files to disks or tape. Assuming the formats are compatible, the disks or tape can be "read" and edited on the second computer. Computers can also be equipped with drives that recognize other formats; for instance, files produced on certain types of Macintosh computers can be read in DOS by an IBM-compatible computer, and the reverse is true—*if* (and don't underestimate the complexity of that "if") the computers have those drives.

The computer gives back the information it's received, using various forms of output devices to let the CAD operator see how the computer is manipulating the data. Usually the CAD operator sits in front of a monitor, which looks somewhat like a television screen.

Another common output device is a graphics plotter. A simple form of graphics plotter may be a dot matrix printer, operating in the "graphics mode," drawing points on a piece of paper, one point at a time. A more complex plotter might use a technical pen which follows the computer's commands and draws a picture on a piece of paper. Sometimes the paper is stationary, and the pen moves in both directions. At other times, depending on the particular plotter, the paper may move in one direction, and the pen may move in another.

Small plotters are standard sheet-carrying devices, usually $8\frac{1}{2}$ inches by 11 inches. Large, computer-driven plotters can even plot on paper as large as 50 inches by 60 inches. Electrostatic plotters work in a similar manner to familiar photocopying machines; they're popular with commercial plotting services and large users, where their immense speed compensates for their high cost. Ink jet plotters work similarly to pen plotters, but use jets of ink which "sweep" across the drafting medium instead of pens.

WHAT THE CAD OPERATOR DOES

A typical CAD operator sits in front of the terminal and keyboard. He or she may be working on CAD with a single standalone personal computer, or at a computer that's part of a local area network (LAN). The mouse, digitizing tablet, stylus, or input device is just inches away, so the operator can reach it easily.

Sometimes a rough paper design already exists for a product. If so, the CAD operator can use the system's digitizing capabilities—the ability to "read" or trace the geometric shape from the paper drawing. Or an operator can use a separate scanner. The computer transforms the information into a series of geometric coordinates, or points, and puts it into its memory. Then the CAD operator can manipulate the drawing on the screen.

Or, perhaps the shape the operator wants is similar to something that's already been CAD-designed. Many companies maintain CAD libraries of files. The operator can tell the computer to retrieve the drawing—or desired details—from the CAD library or from its memory. It's similar to picking out a book from library shelves or calling up a text file containing a previously-keyed-in letter. Once the existing design or detail has been "read" into the computer's memory, the CAD operator can edit it, just as a secretary can make changes in an old letter. When the desired changes in the designs are completed, the edited design can be stored again for later recall.

Typically, a CAD system has a library of designs and commands that have been stored. Much as word processing software has commands already stored that let the secretary delete, re-form paragraphs, or move blocks of type from one location to another in a manuscript, a CAD system contains commands that let the operator erase, redraw, or move portions around the screen. Of course there are also commands that let the operator perform many more functions.

CAD INCREASES PRODUCTIVITY

CAD enhances productivity of designers and drafters because of certain basic functions: replication, translation, scaling, and rotation.

When a product or design has features that are repeated, CAD's ability to *replicate* means the operator can take part of the image and use it in several other areas of the design without having to redraw it each time.

CAD's ability to *translate* means the CAD operator can move images around from one location on the screen to another.

CAD can *scale* by changing the proportions or size of one part of the image in relation to the others, and can zoom in on a desired portion of the drawing, much as a camera lens zooms in for portraits and closeups.

CAD's ability to *rotate* lets the CAD operator move the design around to see it from different angles or perspectives.

And in some more complex 2D CAD programs, CAD can *transform* (or stretch) objects. After the operator has drawn a basic shape, he or she can alter it by relocating selected points (line endpoints, arc or circle centers, etc.) relative to the original. Often, related geometry, such as dimension notes, is changed simultaneously, so it's easy to modify existing designs.

Because CAD systems allow operators to manipulate the images so quickly and effectively, they can accomplish in moments tasks that used to take hours and days with paper and pencil. Those in the field, however, warn that the learning curve for CAD—the time it takes an operator to become proficient at understanding and using the commands—is considerably longer than most people realize. Even those who *know* CAD programs must devote many hours to learning and practicing, as software upgrades and more sophisticated programs are developed.

CAD's *real* productivity, many users feel, is that by automating the routine work of replicating objects, CAD frees up time. "Designers can spend more time actually designing," says point-of-purchase designer Chris Kidd. "Or we can develop designs to a certain point, and give them to other CAD operators to finish the details."

2D AND 3D CAD

Two-dimensional (2D) CAD drawings are rather like an artist's sketch or a drawing made with paper and pencil. For certain applications, such as the design of electronic circuits, 2D CAD is sufficient.

Unlike the real world, the CAD world has what is called $2\frac{1}{2}$D. With $2\frac{1}{2}$D CAD, you can extrude your drawings into the third dimension.

"I can draw a box," says Marmon Pine. "I can project the box as a square into the third axis, but I cannot turn it into a pyramid, since that would alter its original shape. I can make a desk or a book, or can run a cylinder, because the computer moves the drawing down on the Z axis without altering its shape. But it's not true 3D CAD."

The image the operator draws on the computer screen is, of course, two-dimensional (having height and width, but not depth). In the CAD world, however, there is a difference between 2D and 3D. Unlike a paper drawing, a photograph, or a painting, the computer-screen image can be manipulated as if it were a real 3D object. For example, an operator can instruct the CAD system to rotate the object, so he or she then sees another face of the object.

When it's appropriate—and if the company can afford it—there are many advantages to using true 3D CAD in engineering and manufacturing. "The advantage is almost exclusively in the output—what you get downstream," says Bill MacEachnie, who heads the electronic packaging design at Martin Marietta's facility in Orlando.

"2D drafting systems really don't do anything for manufacturing directly," MacEachnie believes. "You still have to look at the drawing. Engineers have to manually develop tooling, setups, and numerical control (NC) tapes, if appropriate, either on-line or off-line. With 3D modeling systems, you can eliminate all that. Using a true 3D system, engineers can take the data directly off the computers and feed it into the machines, eliminating many manual operations. The 3D system also makes it easier to run fit checks and tolerancing checks."

"Some time ago," he recalls, "our company had an in-depth type of projectile that was designed on 3D CAD. When we put it together, we found there was an interference before we built any parts. No one would have caught the subtle tolerance difference without our 3D system. We fixed it and moved ahead. There are gains in 3D, both in engineering and manufacturing, though in reality the designs downstream provide the real savings."

Changing Technology

CAD technology and systems are changing rapidly. The first generation of CAD, 2D CAD, might be described as computerized drafting systems. They reduced traditional dependency on drawings and related paperwork.

HOW CAD AND CAM FIT TOGETHER

Ideally, computer-aided design (CAD) and computer-aided manufacturing (CAM) are parts of a broader concept: computer-integrated manufacturing (CIM).

Many CAD systems can—and do—go beyond computer-aided drafting. CAD lets an operator or designer work out the physical dimensions of the product and the steps necessary to produce it on the computer. Disks containing the information can be used by computer-aided manufacturing equipment. It's also possible to modem directly from the CAD-producing computer to the CAM equipment. However, many companies don't want to risk having data "corrupted"—that is, they need to maintain the integrity of data files, and want to minimize chances that the information could be altered by a glitch in electronic communication. "It's easier and safer for us to Federal Express disks to our suppliers overnight," says a seasoned CAD veteran.

Some CAD systems let the operator "see" the machining process on the screen, and help to guide the operator through various steps in planning the machine process. The system may be able to produce a tape which can be fed into a machine tool controller and used to guide the machine tool path. Under conventional manufacturing processes, a manufacturing engineer would interpret design drawings and establish plans for the machine to make the required part.

In Japan, a major company has developed a process for making customized medical prostheses using a photographic scanner, a PC, and numerically controlled machining equipment. As an example, for a patient with a severe head injury, AutoCAD software is used to "build" a geometric model of the patient's skull from electronically scanned images. Then a mold is designed, creating a precisely matched replacement for severely damaged bone. NC Polaris, a numerical control programming system from an Autodesk company, converts the design into tool path data which guide the production of a perfectly formed prosthesis.

Sophisticated CAD systems are important components of computer-aided engineering (CAE). Of course the CAD system makes it easier to perform drafting and design changes. Engineers can also use CAD systems to visualize how a product will work, or to get an estimate of its performance. Some programs help engineers to perform finite element analysis—breaking down complex mechanical objects into a network of hundreds of simpler elements to determine stresses and deformations.

The solids modeling ability of sophisticated CAD systems, which lets the computer calculate and display such characteristics as the volume and density of the design being drawn, and the finite element analysis capability of such systems, make them extremely valuable engineering tools in major industries like automobile manufacturing and aerospace. Since weight is a critical factor in product design for those industries, 3D CAD systems are a basic part of the technology that lets engineers optimize designs which use the least possible material, while still maintaining strength.

Solid modeling became popular early in the packaging industry, since the volume of highly sculpted containers (like those used for soap or cosmetics) could be determined and monitored during initial design stages. 3D wireframe and solid models can be translated to Rapid Prototyping facilities (stereolithography) for "instant" prototypes. In addition, programs exist which can predict the behavior of plastics as they are injected into a mold-enhancing mold design.

CHAPTER 3

PERSONAL QUALITIES

What personal qualities are necessary to succeed in CAD/CAM and robotics? What do people with jobs in these fields believe you need to do to get ahead? Here's what some of them say:

ATTENTION TO DETAIL

Because CAD and CAM are practical applications of huge databases, a person who wants to make a career in these technologies needs to enjoy working with details. It's important to get things *right*—otherwise, the drawings won't be precise, or the product won't be perfect.

Bruce Bickford, owner of Productive Technologies and himself a CAD veteran, says you'll also need an interest in science. "CAD isn't going to be much fun if you don't want to understand the technology," he warns.

COMMUNICATION SKILLS

If you've been used to thinking of communication skills as your ability to get your point across to someone else, you're right. Those are important, and necessary. But you also need the ability to understand someone else's communications.

"Applicants have to be able to read and understand a manual," says Currin R. Webster, project manager of CAD/CAM/CAE at Bath Ironworks.

Bickford agrees. "Every six months, there's a major update to CAD software," he says. "You've got to be able to pick the new information up quickly, and integrate it into your daily work. You can't fumble through. If you want to get anywhere, if you want to be recognized as a person who gets things done, you've got to be a quick learner."

Asking questions in a manner that elicits answers is an important skill for CAD/CAM personnel who talk with customers. Harold Blanthorn, marketing manager for Berhan Industries, Ltd., a CAD service bureau, says his company develops systems for many of its clients. "Our people have to know how to ask the questions that will get answers from our customers, so we can construct 'how-to's for them," he explains.

INTEREST IN TECHNOLOGY

CAD veterans say there's a complete technology change every three years. People who want to succeed, they say, must be prepared to keep learning . . . to keep being challenged . . . and to look for solutions that may not yet have been invented.

"You need a sense of integrity—a willingness to go beyond your first impression or your first idea when you realize there might be a better solution out there," says point-of-purchase designer Chris Kidd. "You've got to go back if you've finished a job, but you see it's not quite right. If a small segment of a drawing should be round and not square, if you see you need three holes instead of four, you've got to take the time to change your work."

When a customer comes up with an unusual requirement, you need the creativity to find a solution. "If you say you can't do it, but you haven't really tried," warns Philip Farrelly, president of Hudson Control Group, Inc., "you've lost the sale for us. If you tell a customer, 'I don't have the answer,' as far as I'm concerned, that is not a suitable response. At the same time, you can't be a B.S. artist. Customers ask very real questions and need real answers. You need technical expertise and an understanding of the technology."

TEAM PLAYERS

Teamwork is crucial in today's lean workplace. To get ahead, you need to work and play well with others.

"No drawing is ever produced solely by one person," says Blanthorn. "There has to be input, telling you what, how, why, when, and where. A drawing is a graphic reproduction of something you could write in text; it's a set of instructions in pictorial form. Because CAD operators are usually working on the same, or similar, projects, they have to be able to exchange information. They've got to be able to like, or at least tolerate, each other. From a management point of view, we can't afford the luxury of having someone say, 'That guy is such an idiot that when he asks a question, I won't tell him anything.' There's no room for prima donnas."

As companies "rightsize" by eliminating layers of management, as industry moves to flatten out the traditional hierarchical pyramid, the team concept takes on even more importance. "The people who are left will be key individuals who know how to do a specific job," says Webster. "My biggest task is creating user support teams."

Managers today say group dynamics—the ability to work well as part of a team—is equally as significant as the computer skills you need to succeed in CAD/CAM. In the past, U.S. industry was a sequential operation. People designed products, then those products were manufactured. Designers did their drawings, apart from the engineers and workers who actually produced the products.

Today's electronic technology brings people together much earlier in the business, ideally, at the beginning of the design project. Different disciplines—designers, mechanical and engineers, computer hardware and software experts—all work together from the start. Each must recognize the talents and abilities of the other, and be able to recognize others' contributions. A designer may draw a widget, but the production engineer on the team may say, "We can't build that widget efficiently with high-quality production." *Working together,* the team must find answers that are practical in today's world.

CHAPTER 4

CAREERS IN CAD

At the heart of CAD technology is the computer—the data-crunching machine that manipulates figures and digitized points to allow drawing and drafting, refining, and even finite element analysis. But to those with vision, CAD is far more than just a computer program that lets users draft and design.

"CAD isn't an industry," warns Brad Holtz, consultant in computing design and author of *The CAD Rating Guide.* "It's a tool. Whether you want to be in architecture, engineering, or manufacturing, you learn CAD as a tool of your trade. It's as important as being able to write.

"For new people coming into a field, not knowing CAD is a severe handicap."

Being able to use CAD isn't enough to guarantee you a job, however. As Holtz puts it, "Architectural firms are hiring architects who know CAD; they're not hiring 'CAD people.'"

Ten years ago, Josef Woodman, educational manager for AutoCAD at the time, saw CAD jobs falling into five major categories: engineering technologists and architects; engineering managers who needed to know CAD; sales and marketing of CAD packages and services; teachers of CAD systems; and CAD users in factories.

Today that's not necessarily so. As the following stories will show, the routes by which CAD users have gotten to their present positions are indeed diversified. The jobs themselves—and the responsibilities that are part of them—can't be pigeonholed neatly into the categories Woodman envisioned. More and more, that's true, as the lines between technologies blur. Indeed, the job *you* may find in CAD very possibly did not even exist when this edition of *Opportunities in CAD/CAM* was written.

One thing is certain, however. Those who are in CAD and have stayed there enjoy the challenge of this exciting, exploding field.

What's it like to work with CAD? Here are stories of people who do. . .

CAD IN DESIGN ENGINEERING

In 1983, graduating mechanical engineer Bruce Bickford got a job offer when he made his senior presentation. Bickford and his student team at the University of Connecticut had designed a CNC machine that would cut parts. Today, he runs his own business. As owner of Productive Technologies, he still spends 20 to 30 hours of his 65-hour workweek on a CAD system. "Every time a new software package comes out, I have to learn it, along with my employees," he says.

Bickford's initial exposure to CAD came at United Technologies Research Center, where he did mechanical design engineering aspects of jet engines, air conditioners, and elevator parts. He went on to build CAD-designed models for a Mach 14 wind tunnel. "CAD was the only efficient way of doing my 3D wireframe designs," he explains. "They were fairly complex assemblies of 15 to 20 major parts, with complex shapes, complex angles, and canted surfaces.

"I got so wrapped up in CAD that I became a value-added reseller," he remembers. "I sold and supported a number of CAD systems for a couple of years. I broadened my knowledge of the industry and technology, and picked up sales and marketing experience."

Today, Bickford provides design engineering services to clients. He's beginning to move to an offshoot of CAD—computer animation and simulation. "We can do modeling in three dimensions, and 'apply' surface materials," he explains. "You apply textures to various elements of the model. You say, 'I want this part to be metal—or brass—or wood.' The computer generates pictures from any angle or perspective.

A single picture can be outputted on paper or film. If we generate one picture after another at 30 frames a second, we have animation. It's very much like a cartoon is made."

Bickford says that all he has to do is tell the CAD system critical points for key frames. "I want to move a box from point A to point B," he says. "I tell the computer to move the box, and to make that motion happen over 30 frames. The CAD system does all the calculations and produces the animation."

The computer allows him to do special effects that are impossible in the real world—like 'putting' the camera inside a part and having the camera 'look out.'

"The market I'm shooting for is the presentation of ideas," he says. "Someone has a new design. They haven't built it yet. They want to study it, sell it internally, and get a feel for it. An industrial designer may want to check out the esthetics . . . see how the product casts shadows, or put a label on it.

"A second market for me will be to use the technology to help a company with a new concept sell its idea without having to produce any parts. I did 45 seconds of video animation for a company that had a process involving a machine they were designing. They needed to show a prospective customer what the process looked like.

"Another of my customers used my video animation to explain the design of their new patent for a component that goes inside plastic injection molding machines."

Bickford has found his CAD services extremely useful for capital equipment manufacturers—companies that produce heavy machinery for other industrial customers. He serves as the engineering arm of one firm that produces powder coating machines . . .machines that put the plastic on power handles for tools like screwdrivers. Bickford's company also designs and documents subsystems for a firm that makes high-powered CO^2 lasers, used for welding and cutting heavy steel and pipe.

Another of Bickford's customers produces automation equipment for the fast food industry, including automatic french fryers and taco-makers. "The layout of the machines, and the integration of mechanisms and structures, is laid out in CAD, so you can study it in 3D before you have to make any of it," he explains.

Bickford sees CAD as essential—and a highly marketable skill. "Every employer is looking for people with CAD experience," he says. "If you want to go into architecture or civil or mechanical design field, you have to know how to use CAD. People with strong CAD skills are highly valued and represent a real asset to employers."

An interest in technology and science, combined with attention to detail, are "musts," he says. "CAD isn't going to be much fun if you don't want to understand the technology.

"You also need the willingness to advance . . . to try new things. CAD has a complete technology change every three years, and there's a major update to CAD software every six months. You've got to be sharp . . . got to pick up the information quickly."

CAD AND MARKETING

A marketing manager—especially one with a psychology degree—doesn't usually know CAD. But Harold Blanthorn, marketing manager of Berhan Industries, Ltd., a CAD service bureau for clients across the United States, has taught himself the basics. "I started working with mainframe CAD, "he recalls, "but then I switched to stand-alone stations on 386 and 486 computers. I learned hands-on from reading manufacturers' manuals. I took one- and two-day seminars. I exchange information with users groups. I collect information and 'how-tos' and little techniques from others on CompuServe (an electronic bulletin board)."

Blanthorn's point: if you don't understand what the customers your company is servicing are doing, you have problems. "We've all had to re-educate ourselves," he says.

Berhan Industries, Ltd. began more than 20 years ago as a company supplying engineering services to defense-oriented aerospace and electronics manufacturers. Today, however, its design efforts are concentrated in mechanical areas and printed circuit boards.

"We also do a lot of electronic redraw work," Blanthorn says. "For instance, if someone is submitting a product to the Air Force, there may be 800 drawings in desk manuals. Because so many maintenance manuals require schematics and some of the drawings, we'll import those drawings electronically into drawing packages. Then one of our illustrators will sit down and add some shading and possibly additional information."

Because Blanthorn is manager of personnel for the company's CAD services, he and his staff hire a number of CAD operators. "There's no barrier for women or minorities in this industry," Blanthorn says. "Usually there is such a demand that any operator who is competent can find a job."

Here's what Blanthorn looks for:

- Ability to read and understand manuals
- Teamwork skills—both on, and off, the job
- Ability and willingness to follow instructions, without being a hot shot
- Good CAD drawing skills—plus some mechanical knowledge

"We make a religion out of keeping people away from modems and bulletin boards," Blanthorn says. "If we ever deliver a virus-infected disk to one of our customers . . . We tell our people, 'If you fool around with the system, it's grounds for termination.'"

"Operators must know what they're putting on screen," Blanthorn says, "rather than just mechanically performing functions. If they're detailing parts—an entry-level CAD job for us—they must know what a machine surface is going to be, what a finish is, how to show threads, how to dimension properly, and where you're dimensioning from. In other words, they can't just give a dimension between two holes; they have to know where to create a data line to take dimensions from."

Field trips and site visits should be part of a school's CAD training program, he believes. "If we're doing a drawing with concrete and reinforcement bars, it helps to know what the guys in the field will do with that drawing. If you're making a CAD drawing of a square metal plate with three holes drilled into it, it helps if you know how someone in a shop is going to cut that piece of metal to size, put it on a drill press, and drill those holes.

"Then you'll understand that the drill press operator has to know where the center of the hole is in relation to an edge. You'll understand basic dimension principles. What do the people in the shop need in order to actually make what you drew? Did you give them enough information so they can really do their jobs?"

In the Tri-State area around New York City, entry-level salaries start at $280 a week. At Berhan Industries, benefits come after six months. So does a raise—usually to $325 weekly. After that, raises are merit-based. Entry-level CAD operators do a lot of editing, making changes in drawings that can involve text and dimensioning. They master skills such as saving a portion of a block, cut-and-paste, or importing a block into a drawing.

"If they've been absorbing and learning, they're probably making $10–$12 an hour with us after a year," Blanthorn says. "By that time, they're doing simple layout and a higher level of detailing." The next step up is a senior draftsman. "He or she gets a design and breaks it up into subassemblies, taking a section and detailing it. Such a person might bounce between in-house assignments and working on-site at our customers' locations."

The break comes around the $30,000 salary level, Blanthorn says. Some people who don't have the capability of designing stay senior draftsmen; others who can conceptualize become designers.

Such a person could detail or design structural steel, concrete and construction-type plants, or HVAC systems (heating, ventilating, air conditioning). They might design machine parts, aircraft parts, or printed circuit boards. They might design whole complete mechanical assemblies: motors, gears, sheet metal packaging, and front panels, coming up with all the pieces in a shippable unit.

"They may not have an engineering degree, but that's irrelevant," he says. "Competency counts. If they have the ability to sit down and lay out enough on the screen, then they can hand a designer below them a disk that has enough information on the drawing for the designer to finish up what's been conceived." Salaries of these top people can go from $38,000 to $50,000 or $60,000.

CAD IN MANUFACTURING

A CAD System Manager

Doug Speidel is manager of the CAD system for Seagate Technology, a company that designs and manufacturers disk drives for computers. A Michigan State graduate in mechanical engineering, he spent $8\frac{1}{2}$ years at Lockheed, doing mechanical design in CAD systems.

"My interest in CAD started in college when some people from the car industry toured our labs," he remembers. "Then I chose the CAD/CAM option at school."

As Speidel sees CAD jobs, the typical user of a CAD system is a design engineer, often spending 5 to 6 hours a day on a computer, much of it on a $2\frac{1}{2}$D system. Design engineers with the four-year engineering degree start around $30,000, he believes. Those with an associate degree in drafting (usually, from a community college) start at $15,000–$20,000.

During his last three years at Lockheed, Speidel worked with engineers and designers, "trying to find different tools in the marketplace. We looked for software CAD tools and hardware workstations that would help users do their jobs more effectively. I began to work with a whole range of people: designers, engineers, structural analysts like mechanical engineers, or structural engineers who do manufacturing and tooling. The CAD system becomes the hub for all of them. It's a technical hub that people can get data from, share, and use."

At Seagate's Scotts Valley, California, location, Speidel wears two hats. In his job as manager of the existing CAD system, he spends time putting out fires, as well as dealing with administrative issues. "On a recent day, I spent an hour talking to software and hardware vendors," he remembers. "I spent another two or three hours talking to the designers, analysts, and NC program managers in our company. I spent another two hours just managing my own group. The rest of my day was taken up with meetings. I talked to other groups who help us: the group who controls networking throughout the company . . . financial people . . . budget people."

Speidel sees his second function as an agent of change, "making things happen." He's working on technology to pull CAD and CAM together, planning an interface to Seagate's model shop so NC machine operators can use CAD data they get electronically. Getting his master's degree in engineering management helped, he says. "You need management skills. You have to have a thick skin to go out there and help motivate . . . encourage people to change . . . get them to give up comfortable ways of doing things." Salaries are good for jobs like his, Speidel says. "I'm 32 years old, in first-level management with a master's degree and nine years' experience. Industry ranges for people like me are $60,000 to $80,000. There's incredible opportunity for growth in this industry!"

Pete: An Engineering Services Director

Also at Seagate Technology, Pete Diepersloot is senior director of engineering services. As Diepersloot puts it, "I came into the CAD world in 1992, after 25 years in the disk drive industry . . . first as a design engineer, and then as a manager of various functions: development engineering, continuation engineering; test equipment design, logic design, and application engineering support. I'd been a user of CAD systems without ever having had expertise—and there's a steep learning curve to CAD."

Under Diepersloot are several departments: drafting, printed circuit board design, a photo lab, component engineering, a model shop, and the CAD group that Speidel manages. One "customer" of Speidel's CAD group is Diepersloot's own PCB design group.

"We're heading towards being able to do NC machining in our model shop," Diepersloot says. "We're doing prototype work in NC, because we need quick turnaround times. Stereolithography is useful for making 'look-see' models, but typically we make actual functioning parts."

Diepersloot says he's had to come up to speed in CAD in order to speak the language and understand the requirements. "I haven't tried to become a CAD expert user myself; it takes too much time. It's a great career for lots of people, but that's not my job."

What *is* his job, Diepersloot says, is selecting the new tools Seagate Technology will use in the next 2–10 years. "We're working out the transition to dump our mainframe and go to a distributed computing environment," he says. "Our electrical CAD group that designs PCBs has already moved from mainframe software to using Mentor Graphics on Sun workstations. Our next big job is to move our mechanical CAD design tools from the mainframe to the workstation."

Diepersloot is helping choose what hardware platform the company's computers will run on—in short, the computers and the operating systems Seagate will use. "We've preselected a short list of products and vendors in each category," he says. "We're evaluating them and making decisions later this year. We're trying to be a model for other operations within Seagate." The company, which does $3 billion in sales annually, has four U.S. design centers: two in California, one in Oklahoma, and one in Minnesota. In addition, it has offshore manufacturing facilities in Singapore, Malaysia, and Thailand.

Ultimately, once choices are made and budgets are allocated, Seagate will commit the company and its 40,000 employees to those technologies. "Software and hardware are changing so fast," Diepersloot says, "that growth is phenomenal! Over the last eight years, computing power has increased a thousandfold per dollar of investment, and software technology has grown at an equal rate. What we haven't yet learned to do is to take advantage of that increased power and put it to real use to increase productivity. That's what is going to happen."

CAD IN THE MARITIME INDUSTRY

A graduate of the naval architecture program at the University of Michigan, Currin R. Webster combines his lifelong love of boats and sailing with responsibilities as project manager of CAD/CAM/CAE development at Bath Ironworks in Brunswick, Maine. When he joined the company six years ago, he began in its planning and scheduling department, working with new contracts. Two years in the management development program, rotating through various departments, convinced him that "the most exciting thing was the CAD/CAM program!"

CAM is a difficult world, he explains, since computer-aided manufacturing bridges the traditional gap between design and production people. "These two groups don't talk to each other very well," he says. "They often have different procedures . . . different uses for the same information. When you transfer data electronically, you're forced to organize it formally so you capture fields in the same way. Consequently, when you do CAM on a transfer of CAD data, it requires very tight processes."

Much of the company's work comes from government contracts—specifically, building destroyers. "If design were static, things would be easy," Webster says. "But we have a constant amount of change. Because we're designing both manually and electronically, dealing with 3- to 5-year cycles for building ships, our biggest problem is configuration management. If we make a change to the drawing, we must be sure the change is carried throughout and given to the right people."

Today, the company has 200 CAD stations. Each group of a dozen or so CAD stations has a system administrator, who's responsible for the electronic files, making backups, transferring data fields, and making sure the system is up and running. Webster is responsible for all CAD/CAM support development.

"Don't overlook training time when you're figuring CAD costs," he warns. "There's a high cost for initial training, but since CAD systems are being revised constantly, you're constantly re-training people." Webster says AutoCAD is used for 2D drawings. Training starts with a one-week course; within two months, an operator is producing drawings on a regular basis. For the company's ComputerVision system, used for 3D modeling of the ship, initial training lasts six weeks. "It takes at least six months until an operator is proficient," Webster says. "Once they go into training, they're on the system eight hours a day."

Computer-aided engineering (CAE) helps the company extract information from the CAD-designed 3D models of the ship. "We've split the ship into 77 design zones, or buildable units," he explains. "Once that zone is 'built' in 3D, we can do a number of things. We can calculate weight data, in order to distribute the load so the ship floats on an even keel. We can calculate piping and ventilation flow. We can do structural calculations and electrical load analysis, determining how the electrical circuits work and what loads they will carry. We can calculate heat loss per compartment, and can shift calculations for alignment and stress."

Webster foresees CAD/CAM changing the production world. "A lot of the manual jobs, including the drafter and the input clerk, will be eliminated," he says. "The structural engineer will design the structure, check it, and release it to production. There'll be no more middle people.

"Instead, the people who are left will be much more important. They'll need to be more qualified, more versatile than ever. They'll not only have to do their jobs as engineers, they'll need to do cost proposals, training, and presentations to sell ideas.

"They'll need good communication skills, and they'll have to be team players. We're managing much more by cross-functional teams than by hierarchical management."

CHAPTER 5

CAD IN POINT-OF-PURCHASE

The point-of-purchase (P-O-P) industry, which includes everything that's used in stores to display, promote, and advertise specific products, is a $15 billion industry in the United States, and probably $30 billion worldwide. "It's hard to get a handle on real figures," says Rex Davenport, managing editor of *P/O/P Times,* the national news publication of point-of-purchase advertising and display. "There's no single S.I.C. code that covers this industry."

Davenport predicts the P-O-P market will grow rapidly, because the advertising choices that product manufacturers can make are so wide and varied. "It used to be that you could hit the consumer at home during the day with advertising on soap operas," he remembers. "Today, the advertising picture is much more fragmented. Reaching consumers through radio, television, cable, and print is difficult; consequently, reaching them in the store is critical.

"Research shows 66 percent of all buying decisions are made in the store, so having high-quality displays for in-store merchandising becomes even more important."

Increasingly, the behind-the-scenes technology that designs and produces those displays is depending on CAD—and, to a lesser degree, on CAM. That's because CAD has special advantages.

- CAD lets P-O-P designers be innovative, because they can model ideas on screen as well as on paper. Experimenting with new ideas is easy.

- CAD lets P-O-P designers turn designs around more quickly, because CAD lets them make changes virtually on-the-spot to suit clients.
- CAD offers the ability to replicate—to make 24 identical boxes on screen, or to take a space of a certain size and subdivide it, filling each portion with an identical model of a client's product. The designer doesn't have to hand-draw each element in the display.
- CAD designs can be archived. If a design used formerly can be pulled from a library of data files and modified, the designer doesn't have to start again from scratch. CAD is a cost-effective use of a designer's time.

Within the industry, "temporary" P-O-P is the term used for displays that are quickly torn down. For example, a self-shipping display that holds Easter candy for sale will be placed at the end of a drugstore or grocery aisle for a short time before Easter. As soon as the holiday is over, the display will be dismantled. "Semi-permanent" means a P-O-P display designed to last up to six months. Often it's made of plastics, or plastics combined with corrugated materials. Metal clips and plastic bars may be used to give the display more structural strength.

"Permanent" P-O-P means a display meant to last six months or longer . . . often, an acrylic or metal rack, or a hanging display. It's manufactured of more durable materials.

The definitions change, of course, depending on the channel of trade. A corrugated display case at the end of a grocery aisle might last only two weeks if a wet floor mop were used around its base frequently. The same display case in a religious bookstore might last three years because it wasn't treated as roughly.

P-O-P is an industry most people don't realize exists. Yet it can be a place for you to work in CAD or CAM. Here are stories of a few people who do. They find it exciting and wonderful—frustrating, at times, but always a challenge.

P-O-P AND CAD

"The way P-O-P attacks design problems is different from other industries," says veteran designer Christopher Kidd. "The normal, classic manufacturer makes things and then tries to sell them. But P-O-P producers sell ideas—then try to make them."

In the industry, Kidd says he's become identified as "the plastic guy." His complex design for Noxell (with Jim Sweeney, who handled the steel), holds eye shadows, eye pencils, face powders, eyeliners, and nail polishes.

"We used CAD extensively in the development portion of our product," Kidd says. "We did the initial space studies for the product layout in CAD. By taking the actual products and measuring them, we could quickly do up charts showing how things would fit, and what size the modules in the display would need to be."

The Noxell display was made from steel parts and injection-molded plastic parts. "Most of our steel suppliers have computerized systems," Kidd says. "We sent 3D CAD-generated models out on a computer disk for pricing and fabrication. The prototyping and tooling were done from our models.

"The plastic molded parts were done in 2D CAD. Most of our suppliers are small shops that don't have the sophisticated 3D CAD systems. Although we could send our disks to a moldmaker, their CAD programs aren't sophisticated enough to give them a direct translation into CAM for their machining operation."

Kidd, a manual draftsman by training and experience, calls CAD a game. "CAD permits you to design complicated things very quickly by analyzing basic elements and replicating them," he explains. "You see your project as a series of parts that are alike. You design one or two, and then multiply them on the computer."

Because of CAD technology, Kidd and his colleagues say they can offer clients a quick turnaround—12 to 18 weeks is usual in the industry. "From the time a client approves a concept until the displays are built and start being shipped to their sites, we may only have a short time. P-O-P is an advertising industry. If the campaign for a hand lotion kicks off in September, coordinated with print advertising, if we, the makers of P-O-P, don't have those units out there in stores by late summer, we're dead in the water."

As an industry, P-O-P is on the cutting edge of production technology in tooling. CAD generates drawings fast. Because you're dealing with a file on a disk, Kidd says, you can transmit it by disk, by phone, or by overnight shipment of drawings. "Anywhere you want that file to go, it's the same information," he explains. "That gives us tremendous accuracy in communications. CAD gives us a single source for our records."

Lead designer Bill Manifuel, who works for a producer of temporary P-O-P, ties CAD and CAM together electronically. "I'm taking all the designs we are manufacturing and putting them into our CAD system," he explains. "Once we get the design into our computer, we can put additional information in the file. We can designate the exact type wood we use, and the cylinder size we use, and the computer calculates the shrink factor automatically." Manifuel's company sends the files by modem from its computer system directly to the computer systems of its suppliers. He estimates a 15 percent savings on cutting dies—savings that translate into the ability to offer his clients competitive prices.

CAD's big advantages are consistency, cost saving in tooling and preparation time, and the amount of time saved in designing, he says.

West Coast designer Jack Ruszel of Ruszel Woodworks, a producer of permanent and semi-permanent P-O-P uses both CAD and CAM in his shop. "We use AutoCAD in the design stage for renderings or drawings of possible items, so we don't have to build actual prototypes," he says. "If we end up making the job, we use the same drawings we have shown the customer. We take them apart from shop drawings. We have an AutoCAD interface with our NC router. It's more than 20 times faster to program than to plot out by hand. Otherwise, we would have had to do all the drafting, figured where the points are, and had to have written the program for the router."

Steve Young, of the Association of Independent Corrugated Converters, calls CAD "a wonderful tool, with mind-blowing capabilities.

"I can design a P-O-P display on a computer screen, apply the graphics on the screen, do a 3D image on the screen, rotate the image so you can see what the graphics are going to look like on all exposed sides, and show a client what the customer will see as he or she rounds the end of the grocery store aisle. Some P-O-P manufacturers are scanning in artwork. They are actually doing color separations in the computer, and can 'put' the client's graphics in the screen on the computer-generated box."

Young calls CAD a value-added tool in the hands of a good designer. "The box business is a low-profit margin business," he explains. "The more our manufacturers can give clients better design, extra color, or some other specialty—through the use of CAD—the more money they are going to make."

FUTURE USES

Manufacturers of consumer products are beginning to require their suppliers of P-O-P to use CAD and CAM technology. Says Steve Stiffler of Miller Brewing, "Miller Brewing Co. and all our internal departments have made the commitment to use electronics and electronic-assisted programs to improve innovation and efficiency . . . to be on the leading edge of industry. Much of our work is done as a base file. The CAD technology offers the flexibility to eliminate redundancy. We don't have to do things over."

With a CAD data storage bank of files, the company can use the same stored image over and over. Moreover, the data can be shared—not only with design firms, but also with ad agencies, who use the files for pickup photography or product imagery. Miller transfers the information electronically, or by overnight mail.

Another use of CAD is called *planogramming*. Store owners, especially those whose stores are part of a nationwide chain, can draw a grid electronically on screen and "place" products on the grid the way they will appear on the shelves in the store. The technology gives the retailer and manufacturers a way to test the optimum placement of product.

"CAD has been somewhat slow to gain acceptance in the P-O-P industry," says *P/O/P Times'* Davenport. "That's because it's a touchy-feely industry. In the past, the people who have designed displays have been hands-on types who like to cut things out with knives and assemble models.

"Now, design departments and P-O-P producers are seeing what the technology can do. People who are good at these emerging technologies are going to move ahead, as CAD becomes more and more accessible."

CHAPTER 6

CAM JOBS

What opportunities exist for jobs in computer aided manufacturing (CAM)? What is factory automation doing to employment—more particularly, to the qualifications workers need? And what chance do *you* have if you want to work in CAM?

Computer-aided manufacturing varies from industry to industry, and among companies within industries. Different manufacturers are at different stages in their use of automation technologies. Consequently, it is not possible to list all available CAM jobs. Instead, this chapter includes brief descriptions of the technology, stories of several people who work with CAM, and some thoughts on how those in the industry view the future.

One of the best ways to start to get information on automation technology is to subscribe to *Manufacturing Engineering,* the flagship publication of the Society of Manufacturing Engineers. Once a year the magazine runs information on automation, along with lists of vendors in various categories.

Major headings, for example, include: automated assembly, auto-mated-inspection, automatic identification, control systems, CNC machine tools and flexible cells, manufacturing software and hardware, material handling, robots, and sensors.

Each of those headings is further divided into subgroups. Under "control systems," you'll find lists of vendors in NC/CNC/DNC; cell controllers, machine controllers, programmable logic controllers, and robotic controllers. Under "manufacturing, software/hardware," you'll find vendors listed who cover CAD/CAM/CAE software, data acquisition software and hardware, MRP/MRP II (materials resource planning) scheduling software, NC programming software, SPC (statistical process control) software, simulation/modeling software, PCs, micros, and minis, terminals, and workstations.

An alphabetical directory that follows gives manufacturers' names, addresses, phone numbers, and fax numbers. Although, of course, most people who contact companies that are listed are looking to buy products, it's certainly possible for *you* to write for information and catalogs. You can also write to companies listed in the magazine's "free literature" section. Later, when you're actually job-hunting, you'll know something about the companies and what they're selling. And you'll have a list of potential employers to approach.

You can also use the magazine to learn about new CAM products and what they can do. For instance, one sheet metal CAM system automatically selects tools from a library and places them into the turret of a punch press. The system lets users import part geometry from CAD systems. Or they can create the parts from a library of standard and specified shapes. Another CAM software product provides 2, $2\frac{1}{2}$, and 3-axis milling, 5-axis drilling capabilities, and an extensive on-line help system.

Manufacturing Engineering also runs case histories of companies using CAM and related technologies. You can learn a great deal from studying (rather than merely reading or skimming) the articles. For instance, a recent article by senior editor James R. Koelsch described how, at Kennametal Inc., a team of manufacturing engineers from the United States and the UK worked with new product designers from Raleigh, North Carolina, before the firm introduced its KM line of quick-change tooling. Since 1988, the toolmaker has produced the line on flexible manufacturing cells in Cleveland and in the UK.

The article describes in detail the advantages of the cells, which run seven days a week, 24 hours a day. It explains just how worldwide electronic communication ties the team together. For instance, programmers in Cleveland and in the UK use the same McDonnell Douglas Unigraphics CAD/CAM system to create programs. Both facilities have access to 3D models that design engineers have created. Telecommunications technology and networking let workers in the cells reach the host computers to download CNC programs, fixture drawings, part drawings, and inspection instructions.

Studying articles such as this gives you not only an introduction to modern assembly technology, but also a business dollars-and-sense awareness of trends in manufacturing. Goals of the company's cell operation include the elimination of material handling and reduction in work in process. Attendants are cross-trained to be able to operate each machine in the cell, preset tools, schedule work, and help in problem solving.

As Koelsch points out, "The new cell culture also affected production schedulers, supervisors, manufacturing engineering, and quality assurance. *Everyone needed to learn to work differently.*"

Manufacturing Engineering also includes information on new products and their advantages: "reduces small-lot setup time," "fast grinding cycles," "better bandsaw productivity," and "simplifies punch press programing" are typical headlines over product briefs. Through a calendar of coming events, you'll also learn about shows you can attend, such as WESTEC (Los Angeles), and the International Manufacturing Technology Show, advanced productivity expositions scheduled in various locations, a conference on simulation, and another on tube making. Students usually can negotiate an affordable day rate to see the exhibits; attending workshops or conference sessions requires an additional fee.

A number of other trade magazines also cover developments in CAM and factory automation. You'll find them listed in Appendix B of this book, along with information on how to get sample copies. Keeping up with industry news and trends is one of the best ways to monitor the industry.

WHAT CAM IS

Before you can look at the effects of CAM on employment opportunities in today's manufacturing environment, you need to think about what is meant by *computer-aided* manufacturing. As we discussed in an earlier chapter, the U.S. Congress' Office of Technology Assessment says computer-aided manufacturing includes robots, computerized machine tools, and flexible manufacturing systems. Also included are NC and CNC machine tools. All are considered "programmable automation" tools for design, manufacturing, and management. To the extent that a company integrates the system, we say that the company is using *computer-integrated manufacturing* (CIM, pronounced "sim.")

AUTOMATION COMPONENTS

Robots

Many people who'd like to work in manufacturing think a career in robotics sounds exciting. *Opportunities in Robotics Careers,* (2nd ed., 1993) in the VGM Career Horizons Series, also by Jan Bone, takes an in-depth look at robotics opportunities, including salaries, job-hunting techniques, and a detailed look at education and training. You'll also find some of the information in Chapter 7 of this CAD/CAM book. Like CAD/CAM, however, robotics is just one of the technologies that make up programmable automation. If you want a career in manufacturing, you'll need to look at the big picture, rather than specializing too narrowly.

Numerical Control (NC) Machines

In the 1940s and 1950s, numerical control (NC) technology was pioneered and developed by the U.S. Air Force, primarily to help make complex parts for aircraft. Producing reliable tools consistently using manually guided machine tools was difficult. NC technology solved most problems.

Before that time, skilled workers who wanted to cut and form a metal part used a conventional machine tool, shaping the part by hand. They produced the desired shape by moving either the piece being worked on, or the head of the cutting tool. All relevant aspects of the machining process, including the speed of the cut and the flow of coolant, were controlled by the machinist.

In older NC technology, a programmer wrote instructions for the machine at a terminal, which punched holes in a paper or special plastic tape. Next, the tape was fed into the NC controller. The holes represented commands, which were transmitted to the motors that guided the machine tool.

Initially, the NC machine would execute the commands as they were "read" by the tape reader, one instruction at a time. By the late 1960s, entire banks of NC machines were under the control of a single mainframe computer on a time-shared basis.

Both yesterday's and today's machines are considered "programmable." That's because they can easily be set to make a different part when they receive different instructions. Because the machines themselves move their cutting heads and adjust to their own coolants, they are considered automated.

When computers dropped in price and microcomputers became popular in the 1970s, most NC machines got their own computers—one computer to a machine. These computer numerically controlled (CNC) machines let the machine operator edit the program right at the machine, or write programs "off-line," so that factories don't tie up expensive machines while programs are keyed in.

Just as computers have changed since they were originally introduced, so have these machines changed as "new" CNC technology pays off in productivity. For instance, 32-bit processors offer today's CNCs more substantial computing power than earlier machines. Another development in manufacturing teams CNC mills and machining centers with laser digitizers—devices that use laser light to scan structures and turn their measurements into digital signals. Sometimes the data the laser "reads" are blended, through sophisticated software, and eventually exported to a CAD/CAM system. The CAD/CAM system then develops a surface model for machining a tool.

You can learn more about CNC technology by reading *Machining Technology,* a quarterly newsletter from SME's Machining Technology Association. Write SME, One SME Drive, Dearborn, Michigan 48121 for information on getting a sample copy. It's also possible to join SME and the Machining Technology Association as an associate member if you don't have the qualifications of a professional engineer; ask SME's membership department for details.

WORKCELL CONTROL SOFTWARE

CAM technology isn't limited to giant manufacturing companies and huge automated factories. It can work very well in much smaller environments. A firm that spots opportunities and develops niche products to fit a perceived need can be successful.

Workcell control software is a subset of the CAM market. This software makes an electronic connection between working instruments and a larger data system. One of the vendors who offers workcell control software is Hudson Control Group, Inc., a company that specializes in connecting work instruments (including small robots) to larger data systems.

Founder and president Philip Farrelly, who earned a B.S. in civil engineering from Rensselaer Polytechnic Institute and an M.B.A. from Tulane University before serving in the Air Force, says the company developed out of an affiliate of Exxon. "My job at Exxon Enterprises was to find non-oil business opportunities for Exxon," he explains. "Throughout the 1970s, we worked with motor controls and electric control devices. Eventually we began a small business venture within Exxon—selling computer simulators to simulate combustion engineering processes in petrochemical refineries—that the company ultimately decided not to pursue." Farrelly started Hudson in 1983.

Today, the company builds systems for a client list that includes the U.S. Army, DuPont, Colgate Palmolive, Consolidated Coal, Hoechst Celanese, and Mobil Oil. All use small robots in laboratory environments, primarily in quality control applications.

"There's a great need to integrate the robot with other sophisticated instruments," Farrelly says. "You need to be able to communicate with a number of different instruments inside a workcell. For instance, you may have a robot doing tests on whatever you are handling. You also need the ability to date that test data and collect and transmit it across a network to a fileserver. That's not easy to do, using standard programming language."

Under Farrelly, Hudson developed a software package for personal computers which makes it easier for laboratory researchers to control robot systems, and to link numerous devices and instruments together to a single host computer. Earlier versions ran under DOS; now, with a Windows environment, the software has graphical interface and networking capabilities, making it more useful. The computer runs the workcell and exports the data.

"Lots of vendors will write software that provides a host computer interface to the workcell," he says. "They concentrate on graphics, and don't really provide the capability to program. In contrast, our software incorporates a programming language as well as a graphical interface. Our software allows the computer to be set up and perform the duties of an automated workcell. But in addition, our software makes it easy to link various instruments."

In a typical laboratory environment, there are often instruments from different manufacturers. For instance, one device might analyze nitrogen content. Another device from a different manufacturer may measure the X-ray fluorescence of a substance.

"There's a babble of communications requirements in that kind of workcell," Farrelly says. "Our software makes it easy for instruments to talk with each other simultaneously, using different communications protocol." The software contains a graphics builder—a capability which allows the person in charge of the system to produce easy-to-use operator screens. An operator can look at the monitor and follow the prompts; he or she doesn't need much training in how to run the system.

The workcell software Hudson has developed is also used in process control systems. For instance, the software controls a spraying process that puts a hardshell coating on pills of Advil, a familiar over-the-counter pain medication.

Screens (the sequence of information displayed on the computer monitor) produced by the graphics builder "show" the operator what must be done. In addition, the software develops what Farrelly calls a "recipe editor," so the recipes that run the process batch by batch can be edited and saved.

The computer also communicates with a programmable controller that's set to run the process. Hudson's software tells the computer to download process set points—i.e., tell the controller what temperatures are required for successful production—and when.

During production, the temperature in a vessel must reach the desired point and stay there. But there may be more than one set point. The batch recipe for the product may call for the vessel to be at one temperature at the start, and then for the temperature to increase to a higher value within a certain period of time.

A complicated math algorithm (the proportional integral derivative) has previously been entered into the programmable controller. Using the algorithm, the controller "reads" the actual value of the temperature in the vessel, "reads" the desired set point as one of its inputs, and computes what adjustments are necessary to make them match. The controller calculates the volume of gas used to adjust the flame under the vessel, decides how much to adjust the opening on the valve that controls gas flow, and tracks the change in temperature. In addition, the controller sends out all the signals necessary to change the valve opening.

"In short," Farrelly explains, "the programmable logic controller tracks all the instantaneous machine events and controls the process from second to second. The controller maintains continuous contact with temperature and air flow sensors, instruments, and various devices. The host computer, which is running our software, monitors the state of the process through the programmable logic controller. The host computer uses communications technology to 'read' the various values from the programmable logic controller, and transfers those values into a data file that tracks the process."

With Hudson's software, the data file can be printed out into reports. Or it can be networked (using Ethernet) to a material resource planning system or a laboratory information management system.

Typically, both those systems run accounting-oriented programs, so it's not easy for them to get data directly from the production process. Hudson's software makes it easy.

At Lockheed, they've been using small robots in clean room production to build small hypercircuits for the F-22 plane. Now, Lockheed is developing an integrated factory floor, using Hudson's software to link together 15 workcells. "We're providing the interface to different types of production machinery, sending data back and forth from where the production is being done to a fileserver," says Farrelly. That fileserver, in turn, sends its data into a much larger database, loaded with instructions for each of the workcells, depending on the kinds of products desired.

PROCESS CONTROL JOB OPPORTUNITIES

Several types of jobs are available in a company such as Hudson's. Farrelly says there are two sets of technical positions: engineers who are not programming specialists, but who know how to design machinery and electrical systems. "They can make a process control system work," he says. Hudson Control Group also hires computer programmers, able to do "sophisticated" programming, as Farrelly puts it.

Minimum qualifications for both: a four-year degree—with good grades—from a "good" college with a national reputation; Rensselaer Polytechnic Institute, Cornell University, Massachusetts Institute of Technology are examples Farrelly uses. "You don't get into one of those schools without having achieved something, and you don't graduate unless you've survived a tough course," he says.

Hudson hires new graduates or those with one-to-two years experience, and says its pay scale is equivalent to that of Fortune 500 companies. Starting salaries begin about $35,000.

Positions he finds harder to fill, Farrelly says, are sales and marketing jobs.

"It's hard to find good sales people in our field," he says. "That's because many people who get into sales are not good technically.

People who are qualified technically are probably more interested in staying in engineering."

Technical savvy is crucial for Hudson's sales personnel, because they often have to educate the people to whom they sell. "Customers have questions that our sales people must answer," Farrelly points out. "We have to impart confidence . . . confidence that we have the knowledge to come up with answers that will work for their problems."

Hudson's uses recruiters to screen sales candidates, and prefers them to have five or six years' experience. "Our customers aren't going to trust a 22-year-old fresh out of college," he explains. The four-year degree is mandatory, he says. So are good communication skills—for both sales and technical staff. "Although sales leads off, our technical people provide support after the sale has been made," Farrelly says. Tech staff members also write instruction manuals.

"When our people deal with a customer," Farrelly says, "they not only need to understand the customer's needs, but also have a public relations job on their hands when they make a presentation. They must have the ability to make oral and written presentations in English."

EXPECTATIONS OF GRADUATES
ENTERING THE FIELD

College placement officers like Mary Thompson, of Iowa State University, say that companies who interview engineers who are graduating expect them to have had training in CAD/CAM. "It's a given," she says. "But not everyone enjoys it.

"We've had students who dislike it, and students who say, 'I'd be happy to spend the rest of my life in front of a terminal.'" Thompson predicts, however, that since computers are becoming so powerful, some employers will emphasize "virtual reality"—a technology she describes as "intensive CAD/CAM and computer applications of 3D design work."

Two weeks before Iowa State's 1993 graduation, two-thirds of seniors graduating in industrial engineering had accepted jobs, primarily at Fortune 500 companies. "I don't know whether training in CAD/CAM had anything to do with their placement," she admits. "However, our senior design course in the manufacturing technology option incorporates CIM software, so they've had to use it."

Those who'd accepted job offers had a median salary of $33,168—with a low salary of $27,000 and a high salary of $38,000. "Our industrial engineers received salary offers higher than our graduates in mechanical engineering," Thompson says. "It's certainly a viable career."

Regional Employment Outlooks

Job prospects, though, may be less in certain regions of the country. "Engineering graduates with the B.S. degree are having difficulty finding jobs in manufacturing," says Dr. James Luxhoj, associate professor, Department of Industrial Engineering, at Rutgers University. "New Jersey, which had a 9.1 percent unemployment rate in 1993, lost 14,000 jobs in just one month—3,000 of them in manufacturing. Most companies here are downsizing, and engineering positions are becoming hard to get."

"The message to graduates is clear," Luxhoj points out. "Even though you'd like to work in a particular region, such as the Northeast, or even in a specific state, you should broaden your job search. Be prepared to relocate, if necessary, and think nationally when you're job-hunting."

Companies do seem willing, however, to take the cream of the crop. The top student in 1993's industrial engineering graduating class at Rutgers—a young woman—had five job offers, Luxhoj says. She accepted a position with a starting salary just under $40,000. Also on the good side, Luxhoj usually has a dozen students doing summer internships, primarily at companies like Bell Labs, AT&T, Merck, Peat Marwick, and Arthur Andersen Consulting. "Industrial engineering is closely related to management consulting," he points out. "Industrial engineers can help companies integrate and set up CIM and CAM."

At the master's degree level, graduates of the Rutgers Industrial engineering program had a 100 percent placement record in 1993. "Companies are looking for industrial engineers with an advanced degree," he says. "Graduates are primarily finding jobs in systems integration, and with consulting firms who do systems integration as contract work."

Opportunities Following Graduation

Some professors see CAD/CAM as just a specialty, rather than a separate discipline. At St. Cloud State University, Dr. Juan Diaz, chair of the Technology Department, says CAD/CAM is merely a tool in the broad area of manufacturing. "An engineer needs a whole spectrum of competencies," he believes.

However, job prospects are bright for 1993 graduates of St. Cloud's technology program, he says. "Fourteen of the 17 graduates are already working; the other three are interning at average rates of $10 an hour." Diaz sees interning as a valuable way for students to enhance their opportunities. He points out that 10 of the 14 received offers for permanent positions from the companies they'd interned with . . . with salaries ranging from $22,000 to $35,000.

At the University of Missouri-Rolla, Dr. Bill Omurtag, professor and chairman of the Engineering Management Department, calls CAD/CAM "a hot subject."

"Graduates are getting good jobs at all levels—from the draftsman or technician level to the engineer and advanced degree level, all the way up to the Ph.D degree in intelligent manufacturing." In 1993, salary levels for degreed engineers started about "mid-thirties," he says. "Those with a degree in engineering technology may be making $5,000 to $7,000 less, but they're doing very well."

Omurtag sees opportunities for entry in systems integration engineering. "There are many components of manufacturing processes," he explains. "Someone needs to put all of these together with automation. He or she will need to tie machines, conveyors, process equipment, personnel, and inspection together—sometimes with the help of robotics—in order to smoothly and efficiently produce high-quality products."

Many people think that most CAD/CAM opportunities for entry-level graduates will come in aerospace and automotive industries. But Omurtag says that's not true in today's economic climate. He advises those wanting to work in CAD/CAM and manufacturing to look at "packaging" companies—companies in which products are processed, packaged, and shipped, such as General Foods, General Mills, Kraft, and Anheuser-Busch.

Additional opportunities exist, he says, in systems integration companies—smaller, engineering service companies that contract with larger firms to solve those companies' automation problems. "Don't ignore the $10 million-a-year companies," he advises. "That's the wave of the future. That's where you'll find a number of good jobs."

GOVERNMENT-SPONSORED PROGRAMS

More manufacturing jobs, including those related to CAD/CAM, may be down the road as a result of a new government interagency program—Technology Reinvestment Project, part of President Clinton's $1.7 billion Defense Reinvestment and Conversion Initiative. In 1993, administrators of the project began awarding $471 million in contracts, grants, and agreements.

The goal of the project (an interagency effort) is to stimulate the transition to a growing, integrated, national industrial capability which provides the most advanced, affordable military systems and competitive commercial products. To help meet that goal, the U.S. government plans to invest in activities to stimulate the move of existing technologies into commercial and military products and processes, create technologies to enable new products and processes, and integrate military and commercial research and production activities.

In short, the Technology Reinvestment Project is putting money into cooperative research and development, and into operating extension programs to help companies that used to depend on defense contracts to convert to commercial business. Those moneys include:

- $81.9 million for Defense Dual-Use Critical Technology Partnerships. The program's objective: help develop technologies that have both military and commercial applications.
- $42.1 million for Commercial-Military Integration Partnerships. These partnerships will help develop dual-use technology that has clear commercial applications.
- $23.5 million for Defense Advanced Manufacturing Technology Partnerships. The aim: to develop new manufacturing technologies with dual-use applications. A second goal is to significantly reduce health, safety, and environmental processes associated with existing manufacturing processes.
- $43.6 million for Manufacturing Engineering Education Grants. Moneys will support manufacturing engineering education programs at colleges and universities, on a matching funds basis.
- $4.6 million for Manufacturing Managers in the Classroom. Funds will be used to match men and women with expertise and practical experience in manufacturing with colleges and universities. They'll help develop curriculum.
- $87.4 million for Manufacturing Extension Programs. Small manufacturers with under 500 employees will get help in upgrading their capabilities. Like the successful USDA county extension programs, this program will match funds state and local governments commit to deliver services to small manufacturers.

While no one can yet predict the practical implications of this funding on jobs in manufacturing—and, specifically, jobs in CAD/CAM—it should have a healthy effect on U.S. industry. That effect may translate into more and better opportunities for education, for training, and, ultimately, for jobs.

CHAPTER 7

CAREERS IN ROBOTICS

Industrial robots have received a great deal of attention in recent years . . . far more than they did in 1961, when the first industrial robot was used commercially. The vision of an automated factory in which robots and machines work together to turn out products at high speeds is not that far from reality.

Near Grand Rapids, Michigan, there's a "lights out" soap factory that runs 24 hours a day. "Usually no one is in there," says Jim Lakatos, an employment counselor who helps place candidates in jobs related to manufacturing technology. "Robots and automated machinery are doing it all."

As Lakatos describes the plant, railroad cars with materials arrive at one end of the factory. Detergent and additives are automatically unloaded into big bins. They feed through conveyor systems into mixing operations. Once the soap is mixed, it moves automatically to filling machines. Product is pushed into boxes, and a bar code is put on the sides. Automatic stacking/retrieving equipment loads the boxes on trucks that show up at the other end of the factory and depart with product, heading to stores. Although people come in from time to time to make sure the machinery is running smoothly, no one has to be there at any given point. The factory just goes on making products.

Most U.S. factories haven't reached this point, however. A Delphi study of 1984 by the University of Michigan and the Society of Manufacturing Engineers forecast that domestic (U.S.) sales of robots would reach 10,000 units by 1990, and 20,000 units annually by the year 2000.

In the mid-1980s, however, robotics companies hit a downturn in sales. As *Managing Automation,* one of the trade publications that includes news about robotics, puts it, "Reality set in, as the technology's limitations clashed with manufacturers' expectations." Don Arney, division chair, New Technologies, at Indiana Vocational Technical College, agrees that robotics may have been oversold in those years.

"When we first began to look at the robotics field in the early eighties," Arney says, "we felt the growth rate of the robotics industry had been overestimated by a considerable margin. As a result of industry surveys, we discovered that a far more important area of growth was in the general field of automation, where robots were merely another 'automated tool' to be used within the manufacturing endeavor." Based on these surveys, Indiana Vocational Technical College set up its Automated Manufacturing Technology Program—a program which placed 100 percent of its 1991 graduates, at an average starting salary of $19,760.

Although a career in robotics sounds exciting and challenging, how realistic is it to assume substantial opportunity exists?

Robotic Industries Association (RIA), the association of suppliers and users of robots and robotic components, compiles industry figures on use and shipments. In 1991, RIA reported that U.S.-based robotics firms shipped nearly 4,500 robots—the most since 1986. Through the first six months of 1992, new orders received by U.S.-based robotics companies hit the highest mark since 1986, and first-half 1992 shipment totals posted the best mark in five years.

RIA predicts an overall growth of 7 percent in 1993. There are several reasons for this optimism. Economic conditions are expected to improve in the North American market because companies that have been putting off large capital equipment expenditures will no longer be able to delay these investments. In addition, the growing pressure on U.S. companies to improve productivity and product quality requires manufacturing executives in virtually every industry to examine possible solutions.

U.S. Industrial Outlook, 1993, published by the U.S. Department of Commerce, also suggests that the increasing use of robots in the Pacific Rim (countries bordering the Pacific Ocean) and Europe is opening up new export opportunities for U.S.-based companies. There is also optimism about future potential in nations such as Hungary, Russia, Czechoslovakia, and Brazil.

Domestic (U.S.) companies are competitive internationally in such areas as vision guidance for robotics, robot programming and control, and robot sensors. U.S. companies are also strong players in systems integration, a rapidly growing field, for user businesses that increasingly are seeking turnkey automation solutions.

GROWTH IN THE ROBOTICS INDUSTRY

Certainly there is potential growth for robots in the North American market. Donald A. Vincent, executive vice president of RIA, estimates that some 44,000 robots were installed in U.S. factories by June 1992. In fact, some analysts believe that less than 5 percent of the companies in North America that could benefit from robots have installed even one robot.

Vincent cautions, however, that the U.S. robotics industry has "a very long way to go" before robots are sold in the kind of numbers that they should be in North America. "Only in Japan, where some 50,000 robots are installed *each year,* are companies taking full advantage of the productive power of robotics," he says. "It's no accident that Japan is such a strong competitor in so many manufacturing industries—their companies are willing to make a long-term commitment to robotics and advanced automation."

It's difficult to compare statistics because countries define "robot" differently. RIA defines an *industrial robot* as "a reprogrammable multi-functional manipulator designed to move material, parts, tools or specialized devices, through variable programmed motions for the performance of a variety of tasks." RIA uses that definition to track sales and use. The Japanese, however, define *robot* in broader terms.

In the U.S., the largest application areas for new robot orders are spot welding, materials handling, arc welding, and assembly. Vincent says the high number of robots ordered in 1992 for welding indicates that the automotive industry and other heavy manufacturing industries are still the primary customers. However, he believes that orders for materials handling and assembly robots indicate that customers in food, pharmaceuticals, electronics, and other non-automotive industries are helping to stimulate increased demand.

In today's industrial world, robots do far more than work on assembly lines. Robots with grippers perform tasks in such fields as die casting, loading presses, forging and heat treating, and plastic molding. They load and unload other machines. A different kind of robot—one that can handle a tool instead of grippers, or uses its grippers to grasp a special tool—is used in applications like paint spraying; spot or arc welding; and grinding, drilling, and riveting in machining.

WHY ROBOTS?

Many large industrial corporations have begun to move into flexible automation. They've invested in technology and have retrained personnel in order to stay competitive in the global marketplace. Many of them have reduced labor costs substantially—some, to as low as 10 percent of the total cost of production.

Companies such as Motorola have refined a number of their operations to take advantage of automation technology. At Motorola's Boynton Beach, Florida pager plant, robotic "hands" assemble tiny pager components too small for human fingers. Sophisticated software coordinates the operation.

At the company's world headquarters in Schaumburg, Illinois, a tabletop automated factory simulates operations at the Florida pager plant. In an adjacent room, machines "reproduce" a portion of the Florida plant. There, Motorola employees learn how to program robots, solve automation equipment problems, and use advanced technology to design better products.

Robotics technology is also playing a role in defense-related applications. In October 1992, *Robotics and Automation,* the newsletter of the IEEE Robotics and Automation Society, reported that San Antonio (Texas) Air Logistics Center was serving as the center for advanced (applied research) robotics and supporting automation technologies within the U.S. Air Force Material Command. At San Antonio, experts are using these technologies to solve reliability and maintainability problems in supporting existing Air Force weapon systems. In addition, they're working on developing industrial capabilities; on developing hardware and software for rapid prototyping of robotic systems; and leading efforts to develop certification programs for robotic operators and software programmers.

The Move Toward Automation

Several factors may be part of the reason robotics has not (as yet) lived up to early hopes for the technology.

One, of course, is the slump in world-wide economy in the early 1990s. John E. Jelacic, senior international economist, Office of Trade and Economic Analysis, U.S. Department of Commerce, believes world growth will pick up in 1993 to around 2.5 percent, but will stay well below the last peak of 4.3 percent in 1988. Many political and economic uncertainties (including the collapse of the European exchange rate mechanism in late 1992) have led to his cautious outlook. Political and economic turmoil in the former republics of the Soviet Union has also been a contributing factor. In fact, their transition from central planning to market-based, deregulated economies is proving to be slower and more difficult than many had imagined.

In the United States, many small- to medium-size businesses have found it difficult to raise the money needed to modernize and automate. Regulations such as those from OSHA and EPA, the high cost of U.S. labor (and benefits, including health care), and accounting practices that govern how capital investment is reported make it difficult for them to maintain the profit margin to which they've been accustomed.

Industrial robots are expensive. A major drawback is the way in which payback (the number of years the company requires to recover its original investment from net cash flows) is figured.

Automation always involves a capital investment that must be amortized through cost savings on each unit produced. Because investing in a robot may not yield a return for a number of years, a small business may be reluctant to spend the money required to buy it, or unable to convince a lender to finance the improvement.

Another reason small companies have been reluctant to invest is because equipment they have in place may not be being used to its fullest potential. In late 1992, *U.S. News & World Report* estimated that U.S. factories were running at less than 80 percent of their capacity. If factories can already produce more than they are selling, they have little incentive to increase capital spending.

These factors—along with tax laws—tend to slow down the rate at which small- to medium-size companies move towards automation. They affect the numbers of robots purchased and shipped. More importantly, from your point of view, they affect how many jobs there will be which are involved with robotics.

Opportunities in Robotics Careers, (2nd ed., 1993) by this author, outlines the job market and robotics technologies in more detail.

SERVICE ROBOTS

Growth in robotics jobs may come, surprisingly, from a side to robot technology that you haven't heard much about. Robots are used in nonindustrial settings, and their numbers are growing. According to the National Service Robot Association, wherever people want their skills augmented, such as in relieving humans from hazardous jobs, performing security functions, or helping the developmentally disabled, robots are beginning to appear on the scene.

Robotics and Automation reports that since the mid-1980s, 44 utilities have become involved in applying mobile robotic devices to perform potentially hazardous tasks in nuclear and fossil-fired power plants. In fact, according to a survey by the Utility/Manufacturers Robot Users Group, robots have been used in 192 utility-specific applications. Much of the technology has grown out of the use of robots for cleaning up the Three Mile Island nuclear power plant after an accident there in 1979.

Public Service Electric and & Gas (PSE&G) Company, a pioneer in applying robotic devices, says that for every $1 spent on robot hardware, the company has a $2 savings in operation and maintenance costs. In 1990, PSE&G established a state-of-the-art applied research and design laboratory in Hillsborough Township, New Jersey, to test and evaluate new robot designs and prototype of equipment. The facility plans to begin testing security, fire fighting, service, hazardous spill clean-up, environmental monitoring, and various inspection and maintenance devices. Researchers will work closely with vendors to develop and test commercial prototypes.

Growing numbers of robots are used in education, health care, security, training, space, and military operations. Within Robotic Industries Association, a specialty association called the National Service Robot Association (NSRA) represents builders, developers, and users concerned with this application of technology.

"The service robotics industry has the potential to be a very large and important industry in the days ahead," says Jack O'Brien, a veteran of 25 years at Polaroid, who has been responsible there for developing and implementing the company's strategies for sensor development. Polaroid's ultrasonic sensors are often used in mobile robots.

O'Brien believes that key applications for service robots in the coming years are in health care, security, space and underseas exploration, construction, food service, nuclear maintenance and clean-up, and education. Researchers are looking at additional applications. For instance, in the United Kindom, the Department of Trade and Industry's robotics program targets six priority service robot areas: tunneling, construction, underwater, firefighting and security, medical, and domestic.

Service robots are being developed for applications you might never have imagined! Scientists at the University of Washington are working on a mobile robot to handle luggage at airports. Their informal name for the project: Roboschlepper.

The National Institute for Standards and Technology (a U.S.-government-funded agency) has developed a robotic crane they call the NIST Spider. Potential applications in the service industry include excavating and grading. Tennessee Tech's Center for Manufacturing Research and Technology Utilization is working on a tower-climbing robot to paint rusting utility towers.

On the medical side, the Applied Science and Engineering Laboratories of the Alfred I. duPont Institute are studying ways to bring robotic and advanced technology into applications for persons with disabilities. They are concentrating their research on the interface between the human and the machine. A California-based company has petitioned the U.S. Food and Drug Administration, asking them to approve human hip-replacement surgery using the "Robodoc." The robot has already helped perform 25 hip replacements in dogs.

Why Use Service Robots?

Companies that use service robots see them as a cost-effective way of accomplishing tasks. For instance, the health care industry is looking for ways to decrease costs, while still keeping—or even improving—the quality of patient care. Labor costs, especially when benefit costs are factored in, are high. Consequently, hospitals, clinics, and nursing homes are looking at all internal operations, seeking areas where productivity can be increased. Among other issues, they are studying ways to improve "fetch and carry" tasks. It is inefficient, health care administrators feel, to use highly skilled (and highly paid) hospital personnel for these tasks.

As a solution, Transitions Research Corporation, a Connecticut-based supplier, developed HelpMate, a highly sophisticated mobile robot. Helpmate, used in hospitals in Danbury, Connecticut, and Downey, California, is saving money while increasing productivity. "We've been having to pay someone a minimum of $6.65 an hour to go from point A to point B," says a Downey Hospital administrator. "Add to that all of the other normal payroll costs, and it makes sense to invest in a piece of equipment like the robot."

A reduction in workers' hours—with a corresponding saving in costs—is what Danbury Hospital sees as the prime benefit of robot use. "The kitchen has reduced the number of hours we schedule per week from 1,015 to 975," a Danbury administrator says. "The 40-hour savings is a direct result of using the robot."

No one knows exactly what these trends may mean to your future in CAD/CAM, and especially in the robotics side of the industry. Technologies such as machine vision and simulation (and its "cousin," a new software development called *virtual reality*) all hold promise. You will want to monitor developments closely to see what implications they have for the career choices you will be making.

CHAPTER 8

EDUCATION AND TRAINING

What do you need to get a job in CAD/CAM? Where should you go to school? What should you study?

You may be able to start right now!

Today, in an increasing number of high schools, CAD has completely replaced courses in manual drafting. At some of these schools, CAD sequences are offered. For instance, in Arlington Heights, Illinois, a Chicago suburb, students at John Hersey High School can take up to four years of CAD training as elective courses. "Our introductory course exposes students to CAD, using AutoCAD software," explains John Hangey, head of the school's practical arts division. "They learn to manipulate simple objects."

As students progress through the sequence of courses, they increase their CAD proficiency. Two tracks are offered: an architectural program, and an engineering program.

Students at nearby Wheeling High School, part of the same high school district, learn CAD in a state-of-the-art technology lab. As part of its Center for Applied Technology, the school has developed 20 different modules—most, six days long. Students work in pairs, rotating through the modules. The high school uses 12 CAD stations with 2D CAD software for its architectural and engineering drawing courses, and plans to upgrade to 3D CAD as soon as funds are available.

"I've had my high school students get part-time jobs in CAD," says technology education teacher Dennis Mueller. "Nearby engineering firms will occasionally hire them to do modified drawings—at $10 an hour."

Several graduates of the Wheeling program have gone on to receive further training in CAD programs at nearby William Rainey Harper Community College and at Illinois State University, he says. "There's a real need for well-trained persons who know CAD. In fact, Illinois State's industrial technology program placed all its 1993 graduates, at an average starting salary of $26,000; the top graduate started at $40,000."

Mueller himself stays in close touch with nearby employers, such as Motorola, to be sure the high school students he teaches are receiving the kind of training that industry needs. At Wheeling High, that can also include exposure to CAM. The school has computer numerically controlled (CNC) software and machinery.

But Mueller sees CAD, rather than CAM, offering more potential for jobs. "The average manufacturing firm is moving from desktop drawing to CAD," he points out. "However, it's common to have a tool and die shop that's converted to CAD, but still has people doing prototyping, replacement and machine parts. Many small manufacturers are job shops. They aren't doing things with CAM because they aren't making large quantities of the same products."

It's certainly realistic to expect that you may be able to find part-time work, even as a high school student, if your CAD technical skills are good, if you market yourself aggressively, and if—once on the job—you continue to learn. But if you *really* want to succeed in tomorrow's workplace, you almost certainly will need additional skills. Increasingly, experts are recommending a series of specific "I can do" competencies as a necessary ingredient for moving up.

SCANS

In 1991, the Secretary's Commission on Achieving Necessary Skills (SCANS) was appointed by the U.S. Secretary of Labor to determine the skills people need to succeed in the world of work. The Commission's purpose: to encourage a high-performance economy, characterized by high-skill, high-wage employment. Its members, distinguished leaders from education, business, labor, and government, were charged with defining a common core of skills that constitute work readiness for the jobs of today and tomorrow.

SCANS reports have identified "workplace 'know-how'"—made up of five workplace competencies and a three-part foundation of skills and personal qualities that are needed for solid job performance.

Here are the Workplace Competencies SCANS says effective workers can productively use:

- Resources—They know how to allocate time, money, materials, space and staff.
- Interpersonal skills—They can work on teams, teach others, serve customers, lead, negotiate, and work well with people from culturally diverse backgrounds.
- Information—They can acquire and evaluate data, organize and maintain files, interpret and communicate, and use computers to process information.
- Systems—They understand social, organizational, and technological systems. They can monitor and correct performance, and they can design or improve systems.
- Technology—They can select equipment and tools, apply technology to specific tasks, and maintain and troubleshoot equipment.

Here are the Foundation Skills SCANS says competent workers in the high-performance workplace need:

- Basic Skills—reading, writing, arithmetic and mathematics, speaking, and listening.
- Thinking Skills—the ability to learn, to reason, to think creatively, to make decisions, and to solve problems.
- Personal Qualities—individual responsibility, self-esteem and self-management, sociability, and integrity.

This combination of workplace competencies and foundation skills—SCANS calls it "workplace 'know-how'"—is not taught in many schools or required for most diplomas. Nevertheless, your chances of succeeding in CAD/CAM or a related career are better if you can perform the tasks identified in the SCANS reports.

You'll almost certainly improve those chances if you have post-high school training. Once, a high school diploma was a sure ticket to a job; today, however, the market value of that high school diploma is falling. The SCANS report *Learning a Living: A Blueprint for High Performance* says the proportion of men between the ages of 25 and 54 with high school diplomas who earn less than enough to support a family of four above the poverty line is growing alarmingly.

In 1989, more than two in five African-American men, one in three Hispanic men, and one in five white men—all with high school diplomas—did not earn enough to lift a family of four above poverty. Unless there is a second wage earner, their families will not have what most would call a decent living.

The workplace "know-how" SCANS has defined is related both to competent performance and to higher earnings for the people who possess it. When the "know-how" required in 23 high-wage jobs is compared with the requirements of 23 low-wage jobs, SCANS says, workers with more "know-how" command a higher wage—on average, 58 percent, or $11,200 a year, higher.

If you do have the SCANS competencies, if you do have a degree or advanced course work, if you do have experience in an architectural firm or engineering-related jobs, can you get hired in CAD/CAM?

"Yes," say most experts, "at least, in jobs that require CAD skills." They have several reasons for their positive attitude. "More and more smaller firms in architecture and engineering are converting their files and drawings to a CAD format," says John Hangey, division head of practical arts for John Hersey High School in Arlington Heights, Illinois. "In order to compete, those firms are having to go to the more efficient CAD system, rather than the old manual way of drawing."

In addition, Hangey says, the move toward a global economy is hitting CAD users. "The prints and drawings which are made in the United States may wind up being used to build or assemble a product in Hong Kong," he points out. "CAD provides the universal language users need to transcend geographical boundaries."

Hangey and Mueller both say CAD training is essential for architects and those who work with them. However, they predict CAD jobs will be easier to find for those who have engineering-related training. "That's because there's much more going on in manufacturing," Mueller explains.

ABET

If you are interested in the engineering side of CAD—and that's where more of the jobs seem to be—you will want to know about the Accreditation Board for Engineering and Technology, Inc. (ABET). For over 60 years, ABET has been monitoring, evaluating, and certifying the quality of engineering and engineering-related education in colleges and universities in the United States. ABET develops accreditation policies and criteria. The board runs a comprehensive program that evaluates engineering and engineering technology degree programs. Programs that meet ABET's criteria are granted accredited status.

The U.S. Department of Education formally recognizes ABET's exclusive jurisdiction for accrediting engineering, engineering technology, and engineering-related education. In addition, state licensing authorities—either by specific statute or by long-standing practice—generally recognize ABET-accredited engineering programs for full educational credit towards satisfaction of state Professional Engineer licensing requirements. Graduates of ABET-accredited programs have a high degree of job mobility, because of the wide recognition of the accreditation system in the world engineering community.

ABET defines *engineering* as the profession in which a knowledge of the mathematical and natural sciences gained by study, experience, and practice is applied with judgment to develop ways to utilize, economically, the materials and forces of nature for the benefit of all people.

ABET defines *Engineering Technology* as that part of the technological field which requires the application of scientific and engineering knowledge and methods combined with technical skills in support of engineering activities; it lies in the occupational spectrum between the crafts worker and the engineer at the end of the spectrum closest to the engineer.

ABET defines *Engineering-Related Programs* in higher technical education as mathematics-and-science-based programs that do not fit the strict definitions of either engineering or engineering technology, but have close practical and academic ties with engineering. With appropriate participation from societies representing specific engineering-related professional disciplines, engineering-related programs may be structured to prepare graduates into professional practice in a discipline that is neither engineering nor engineering technology (for example, surveying and mapping, or industrial hygiene).

Each year, ABET issues its annual list of accredited programs. In addition, ABET publications, which can be ordered for a fee, include an annual report, and publications on engineering accreditation, engineering technology accreditation, engineering ethics, professional development, continuing technological education, and accreditation of engineering-related programs.

A 10-minute videotape cassette is available from ABET. "Engineering and Engineering Technology—Accreditation for Quality Education" provides a description of ABET's accreditation process and the benefits of accreditation to institutions, students, employers, and the engineering profession.

For further information, write to ABET, Publications Office, 345 E. 47th St., New York, NY 10017-2397.

TRENDS

As you begin to plan your career in CAD/CAM, especially if you are emphasizing manufacturing technology, there are several trends you'll have to monitor. Hangey's point about a global economy is well-taken. Offshore sourcing—in which companies put together parts and components overseas, where production costs are lower—has become a significant factor in today's manufacturing.

It's not only U.S. manufacturers who have jumped on the bandwagon. In 1993, *Business Week* reported that German manufacturers had dropped 500,000 workers in the preceding 12 months as a protest against Germany's average $25.21-per-hour production costs. "Germans are opening plants in eastern Europe, China, and South Carolina to tap into cheaper labor, serve faster-growing markets from local bases, and concentrate domestic efforts on high-technology goods," the magazine said. "Executives, engineers, and factory workers alike are rethinking the entire way they design, produce, and market everything—from cars to environmental clean-up gear."

Another trend you'll need to watch is the move towards concurrent engineering as manufacturers rethink the traditional design process. As Harold J. Raveche, president of Stevens Institute of Technology, puts it, "Automated concurrent engineering propels U.S. industrial competitiveness decades ahead of other nations by bringing products to market in half the amount of time and with superior quality." A software-based system developed at Stevens shortens research and development cycles, eliminates costly design flaws, improves product quality and reliability, and reduces costs. "This method will allow U.S. industry to leapfrog our international competitors in product manufacturing," Raveche says.

Synchronous manufacturing is a third trend you should watch. The terms refers to a time-based competitive strategy that focuses on moving material through a factory more quickly. General Motors committed its entire company to the concept in 1992 as a way of carrying inventory off its balance sheets and on to those of its suppliers. GM also suggested to its suppliers that it would be prudent if they also adopted synchronous manufacturing in order to keep pace with GM's rate of change and improvement.

Simulation—computer software that makes it easier for engineers to answer "what if" questions—is also becoming widely used by companies with high-value manufacturing programs. By 1993, reports *Industrial Engineering,* "simulation within a manufacturing or assembly environment was being used routinely in situations involving new construction, and whenever there was a model changeover." Detailed, real-time simulations can recreate the movement of materials and products on screen and on printout as that movement would occur under actual production conditions.

Simulation software can be combined with CAD systems to help companies meet rapidly changing production requirements. For instance, WITNESS, a simulation software from AT&T ISTEL, can be combined with AutoCAD, the leading software for personal computer-based CAD. Users can modify an existing plant or build a new one, and can simulate processes—all on screen.

Global Economy. Concurrent engineering. Synchronous manufacturing. Simulation. They're big terms, and big concepts. Why is it important *for you* to monitor them if you want a job in CAD or CAM?

Because today's manufacturing methods are changing so quickly, because businesses are rethinking traditional methods and processes, because trends like those listed above have implications for the number of jobs available, you yourself are going to have to take a much more active role in planning your career than might have been the case several years ago. You can't wait for a counselor or professor to predict what is going to happen. You'll have to read the business periodicals and the trade magazines. You'll need to decide for yourself how best to modify your training so you'll be able to compete effectively in the job market.

Specifically, the trend towards the global economy and offshore sourcing means that someday you may work overseas, using CAD, CAM, or both technologies. Your coworkers may be locally hired and trained, or you may work in the United States at a company owned by a foreign corporation. Either way, the employee who has fluency in a second language, who is aware of cultural diversity, and who understands how to work effectively in a multi-cultural team—and who also has sophisticated CAD and CAM skills—has a far greater chance to move up than a worker who's proficient in CAD/CAM, but who doesn't see the big picture.

The push for concurrent engineering means you may be using CAD and simulation tools to design in safety and efficiency up-front, before a product is ever made. According to Boeing's Ken Drew, the company has a sophisticated computer program, informally nicknamed "Robbie the Robot." Robbie lets engineers use CAD-related software to design a human model. During the designing of Boeing's new 777, engineers "put" that human model at virtually every place in the aircraft in order to discover how well a person would be able to do maintenance or repair work. Necessary design modifications, made upstream, saved Boeing time and money.

Synchronous manufacturing and simulation also are related to potential CAD-related jobs. Since "work-in-process inventory" (a term used in cost accounting for the cost of uncompleted goods still on the production line) doesn't produce money for a manufacturer, any method (including CAD) that speeds up a factory through-put helps the company's bottom line.

RESEARCHING EDUCATIONAL OPPORTUNITIES

CAD and CAM in Architecture and Design

Where should you go to study CAD and CAM? What courses should you take?

If you'd like to study CAD with the idea of a career as an architect or designer, there are several ways you can find schools that emphasize such courses.

You can ask your school or public librarian to do a computer search of Dialog, an information-providing service, using a database called "Peterson's." Once the librarian is on-line, he or she can do a subject search for you, using "computer-aided design," "computer-aided drafting," "CAD," and other related terms to get a list of schools.

Another way to locate information is to consult the *College Blue Book,* published every two years, and almost certainly on your library's reference shelves. Look for the volume titled "Degrees Offered by College and Subject." Under "computer-aided design and drafting technology," you'll find schools that teach it. Your librarian can help you get addresses for the schools. Then write to them directly.

One of the most effective ways to get school, training, and career information is to consult the *Encyclopedia of Associations,* published annually by Gale Publishing, Detroit. The volumes are indexed in a unique way; read directions on how to look things up, or ask your librarian to explain the procedure. Check listings of national associations for architects and designers. Usually associations will have career information, as well as material on schools and colleges that offer programs. Write for information.

CAD and CAM in Manufacturing

One of the most effective ways for you to research information on this option is to buy the *Directory of Manufacturing Education.* It's affordably priced and available from the Society of Manufacturing Engineers, One SME Drive, Dearborn, Michigan 48121-0930. Included in the comprehensive directory is information on over 550 colleges, universities, and technical institutes that have degree programs in manufacturing and related areas—including courses in CAD and CAM. Listings include degrees and course offerings; cooperative education and evening programs; and complete names, addresses, and phone numbers of persons to contact.

ABET-accredited manufacturing programs are indexed. So are programs at colleges with associate degree programs, bachelor's degree programs, and master and Ph.D.-level degree programs.

PROFILE 21

As you research these programs, it may be helpful to know the findings of an SME study (Profile 21), commissioned to determine what the manufacturing engineer's job description would look like by the year 2000. Key findings included the following:

- "Manufacturing engineers will function increasingly as operations integrators. In other words, they'll help to coordinate people, information, and technology within an organization."

SME says this means that many manufacturing engineers will need to emphasize management and business skills over scientific and mathematical skills in their ongoing professional development.

- "Given the growing overall importance of the manufacturing engineer's increasingly complex tools to everyday planning, logistics, and work flow, he or she must assume a greater role as strategist."

In short, many manufacturing engineers will need to deal with problems and solutions—not only in technological and logistical ways, but also in terms of the end user in a shifting global marketplace.

- "Teamwork and people skills will play an increasingly important role in the work of manufacturing engineers."

Consequently, manufacturing engineers will need to know how to recognize individual skills and points of view of employees at all levels. That's a crucial skill, says SME, if companies want to stay competitive in the future manufacturing environment.

You can find out more about manufacturing engineering (a career that often includes jobs related to CAD, CAM, or both) by watching any of several award-winning video programs. They're available free of charge to schools, libraries, and career counselors.

Videos are: *Challenge of Manufacturing,* intended for junior or senior high school students ages 12–19, features people working as manufacturing engineers producing bicycles, blue jeans, compact discs, and cosmetics. *Race Against Time,* designed for persons ages 15 and up, provides information for people evaluating manufacturing as a career path. The program explores the status of manufacturing, new strategies in use, competition, teamwork concept, and the rewards of manufacturing. *Engineering: Making It Work* emphasizes how manufacturing touches our lives in everything we do, from music to make-up, cars and clothing, jet fighters and rock and roll. It's suitable for all ages and grade levels.

While none of these videos specifically targets CAD/CAM as a career, nevertheless, each shows the factory environment and discusses activities young people can do while they are still in high school to help prepare them for manufacturing engineering. Career brochures and posters can also be purchased for use with the videos. They promote manufacturing education to teachers, students, and professionals.

Contact the SME Education Department, One SME Drive, Dearborn, Michigan 48121 for free loan or for purchase information.

Finally, one of the most important things to remember about CAD and CAM is that each is just one part of technology used in automation. Both need to be looked at as part of a larger system, rather than as stand-alone technologies. "I would not recommend that a student pursue a career just in CAD/CAM," warns Dr. J. T. Black, from Auburn University's Advanced Manufacturing Technology Center. "It's too narrow. Instead, many of the jobs are in learning how to apply CAD and CAM in manufacturing environments."

APPRENTICESHIPS

Apprenticeship is another way in which occupational training takes place. Today, apprenticeship is a businesslike system designed to provide workers entering industry with comprehensive training that exposes them to practice and theory. Generally this training is a combination of structured on-the-job "how to" and related theoretical information.

In the United States, the government defines an apprentice-able occupation as one that is usually learned in a practical way through a structured, systematic program of supervised on-the-job training. The occupation involves manual, mechanical, or technical skills and knowledge that require a minimum of 2,000 hours of on-the-job work experience.

U.S. apprenticeship programs, which are voluntary, are operated by employers, employer associations, or jointly by management and labor. The National Apprenticeship Program is the term used to describe the coalition of management, labor, and government that supports the apprenticeship program in the United States and all such programs nationwide.

The U.S. government provides support services to sponsors of apprenticeship programs. Under the National Apprenticeship Act, the Bureau of Apprenticeship and Training (part of the U.S. Department of Labor) is responsible for providing service to existing apprenticeship programs. The Bureau also provides technical assistance to organizations that would like to set up apprentice programs. The Bureau works closely with State Apprenticeship Councils and the educational system.

Federal and state apprenticeship agencies recognize over 800 occupations as apprenticeable. While CAD/CAM isn't one of them, such related occupations as Architectural Drafter, Electronics Technician, and Engineering and Scientific Programmer are listed. Write to the nearest agency for information. You'll find a list in Appendix C of this book.

STAYING ABREAST OF CHANGING TECHNOLOGY

Technology in CAD/CAM and related fields is changing so rapidly that you'll need to keep up, even though you're working in the field. There are several ways you can do this.

Conferences. Many of the major associations have exhibitions at which vendors display the latest in hardware and software. Usually these exhibitions are tied into major conferences. Students can generally view the exhibits for a reduced fee, and may be able to attend workshops at a student discount.

Major conferences include a number of shows during February or March, each tied to National Manufacturing Week. You'll find registration information in *Plant Engineering,* the trade magazine that acts as show sponsor. Autofact (the automated factory show) is held each

November. It's sponsored by the Society of Manufacturing Engineers (SME). SME sponsors other major shows, including the International Manufacturing Technology Show. Registration information is carried in *Manufacturing Engineering,* the SME trade magazine. You can get a complete calendar of SME-sponsored upcoming events by contacting SME at One SME Drive, Dearborn, Michigan 48121. The calendar is also carried online by SME's bulletin board; get modem parameters from SME.

The Institute of Industrial Engineers sponsors a major annual conference with preconference seminars, as well as a number of meetings, held at various locations around the United States. Read *Industrial Engineering* for details, or write the Institute of Industrial Engineers, 25 Technology Park/Atlanta, Norcross, Georgia 30092.

Chapter Meetings. Trade associations like SME and IIE have chapters in major cities. Guests can almost always attend a single meeting for a low fee. Regular monthly meetings feature speakers, and often include plant tours. Attending meetings (and becoming active in a chapter) are good ways of getting contacts that may later lead to employment.

Self-Study. All the trade associations listed in Appendix A of this book publish papers, journals, and books. Buying and reading those in your particular field of interest will help you keep current on technology, as well as on the nontraditional issues facing today's CAD/CAM personnel. As Eric E. Torrey, editor of *Industrial Engineering,* points out, "Non-traditional jobs are becoming available for industrial engineers because IEs are taking their traditional tools and applying them to new problems and new technologies." Such areas as sales, marketing, and finance may provide job openings for those with technical training. Maybe one of those jobs will be yours!

Vendor-Sponsored Courses. Most major vendors of CAD and CAM software have seminars as part of their customer education programs. Usually an employer will pay your fees, but individuals with prerequisite training are welcome to attend.

For instance, ComputerVision, a company that makes CADDS software, offers courses at Bedford, Massachusetts; Chicago; Dearborn,

Michigan; and Marina del Rey, California, scheduled at various times throughout the year. A typical offering is a one-week course in "Basic Mechanical Design," planned for mechanical engineers, designers, and detailers who create or use mechanical design products. Prerequisites were a ComputerVision tutorial in "Introduction to Solid Modeling," plus 120 hours of CADDS 5 system experience. Topics covered included documenting solids; basic entity creation, modification, and manipulation; Boolean functions; filleting and sewing solids; get data techniques; and construction planes. For information, contact ComputerVision, 11 Oak Park Drive, Bedford, Massachusetts 01730.

LICENSING AND CERTIFICATION

If you want to work in CAD or CAM, no license or certification is needed—just competency. However, if you want to practice as a professional architect or engineer, you will need to be licensed by the state in which you work.

For information on requirements, you'll need to contact your individual state government. In Illinois, for example, look for the Department of Professional Regulation. However, the name of the agency that handles registration and licensing isn't the same in every state. You can find out the name of the department by phoning directory assistance for your state's capital city. You can also look in *State Executive Directory,* a quarterly publication by Carroll Publishing Company, available at the reference desk of most public libraries.

Other sources of information are the American Institute of Architects, 1735 New York Avenue, NW, Washington, DC 20006, and the Accreditation Board for Engineering and Technology, Inc. (ABET), 345 E. 47th St., New York, NY 10017-2397.

The National Institute for Certification in Engineering Technologies (NICET) issues certificates to engineering technicians and technologists who apply for certification and who satisfy competency criteria through examinations and verification of work experience. More than

78,000 technicians and 700 technologists have been certified. For information, write NICET, 1420 King St., Alexandria, Virginia 22314.

SCHOOLS AND COLLEGES

Here's a sampling of schools and colleges offering course work in CAD/CAM, usually as part of a larger offering in manufacturing technology.

College of DuPage. This community college provides education in automated manufacturing. Within its Occupational and Vocation Division, the college offers two programs: one in Electro-Mechanical, and the other in Manufacturing Technology, which lead to the Associate of Applied Science degree or to one of the numerous certificates.

Course work stresses practical applications of technology, and offers extensive hands-on laboratory experience. Programs also contain courses in process control, programmable controllers, drafting, numerical control, and CAD/CAM technology. Co-op and job training programs are also available. For more information, contact College of DuPage, 22nd St. and Lambert Rd., Glen Ellyn, IL 60137-6599.

Eastern Illinois University. The Manufacturing Technology option of the Industrial Technology degree program in the School of Technology is designed to prepare individuals to meet the challenge of the modern domestic manufacturing industry. The option focuses on a state-of-the-art manufacturing system that includes computer-aided design (CAD), computer-aided manufacturing (CAM), computer integrated manufacturing (CIM), and robotics. Courses in these areas, in combination with other management and engineering-related courses such as Manufacturing Management, Plant Layout and Material Handling, Statistical Quality Control, Machine Design, Work Measurement and Method Design, Materials Technology, Statics and Strengths of Materials, and others prepare specialists to manage automated manufacturing systems.

Job titles reported by graduates include Manufacturing Engineer, Production Control Manager, Engineering Technician, Applications

Instructor, and Operations Manager—as well as other positions of responsibility in management and engineering-related areas. For more information, contact The School of Technology, Eastern Illinois University, Charleston, Illinois 61920.

The Center for Intelligent Machines And Robotics (CIMAR), at the University of Florida in Gainesville, has a Machine Tool Laboratory that develops and tests milling machines. Research into NC programming for quality in machining and the creation of comprehensive supervision systems for machining centers are just a few of its projects. Funding for research projects has come from the National Science Foundation; from General Motors, Carrier, Magnetic Bearings, Inc., Ford, and Selco; and from the U.S. Air Force. Other research projects include the development of advanced robotic systems that can do maintenance and repair tasks in nuclear power plants. For more information, write CIMAR, 300 MEB, University of Florida, Gainesville, Florida 32611-2050.

Gateway Technical College has a two-year associate degree program, "Computer Integrated Manufacturing Technician." In 1992, two-thirds of graduates from that program who were surveyed were working in related occupations; the remaining third were employed. Their hourly wage for those who were working full-time averaged $11.91. Three-fourths of graduates from Gateway's two-year associate degree program in Electromechanical Technology (Robotics) were working, and more than half of those had jobs related to the program. Their average hourly wage was $10.62.

Graduates of the Computer Integrated Manufacturing Program are finding entry-level jobs as computer integrated manufacturing engineer/technicians; manufacturing engineering technicians; robotic specialists; and manufacturing technicians.

For more information, contact Gateway Technical College, 1001 South Main Street, Racine, Wisconsin 54303-9610.

Indiana State University. The program in Computer Integrated Manufacturing (CIM) Technology prepares graduates for technical and supervisory positions in Computer Aided Manufacturing (CAM) and

Computer Aided Design (CAD). Students take course work in such areas as machine tool fundamentals, materials and processes, design drafting, production planning and control, and quality control. Graduates have the competency to fill positions in manufacturing that involve computer numerical control (CNC) machinery, robotics, automated systems control and interfacing, computerized operations scheduling, and data communications information and control systems.

For more information, write Department of Manufacturing, School of Technology, Indiana State University, Terre Haute, Indiana 47809.

Iowa State University has computer and laboratory facilities that use computer-integrated manufacturing. It offers a cooperative program that combines education with on-the-job engineering experience. Students in industrial and manufacturing systems engineering—27 percent of whom are women—graduate with a Bachelor of Science degree in Industrial Engineering. At graduation, they are fully prepared to take the registration exams that qualify them as registered professional engineers.

The school's philosophy is that computer integrated manufacturing (CIM) is essential to the survival of American industry in the 1990s and beyond. In the context of CIM, manufacturing includes product design as well as production, assembly, and distribution activities. All these elements are integrated by computers—resulting in a totally controlled system.

Core industrial technology courses include Computer-Aided Design (CAD) and courses in Manufacturing Automation. In a typical CAD course, for instance, students will explore three-dimensional transformations, wireframe models, 3D projections, and basic parametric representations of curves, surfaces, and solids. A course in computer-aided manufacturing would discuss the use of computer technologies in planning and controlling manufacturing processes, computer numerical controls, CNC programming languages, and CAD/CAM integration.

For more information, write College of Education, Department of Industrial Education and Technology, 114 I. Ed II, Ames, Iowa 50011-3130.

Lima Technical College allows students to major in Flexible Manufacturing Systems as part of its two-year associate degree program. Graduates can program CNC machine tools, robots, programmable controllers, and computers. CAD and CAM are also part of the program. For more information, contact Dean, Engineering Technologies Division, Lima Technical College, 4240 Campus Drive, Lima, Ohio 45804.

Lorain County Community College, also in Ohio, offers a two-year associate degree in automation engineering technology. Industrial robotics and computer-integrated manufacturing are just two of the required courses. The ATC CIM Laboratory, a fully automated flexible manufacturing cell, uses computer-integrated manufacturing techniques. Full-size automated machining equipment, two CNC machines, and robots are part of the laboratory. For additional information, write Lorain County Community College, 1005 North Abbe Road, Elyria, Ohio 44035.

North Iowa Area Community College offers a 2-year Associate of Applied Science degree program that prepares students to install, maintain, program, troubleshoot, and service high-tech systems found in computer-automated manufacturing facilities. Graduates find work as technicians in systems/maintenance, instrumentation, electromechanical and control systems, and robotics, and in computer-automated process control. For more information, write North Iowa Area Community College, 500 College Drive, Mason City, Iowa 50401.

Northern Kentucky University has associate and bachelor's degree programs in industrial technology, and bachelor's degrees in manufacturing engineering technology. Both degree areas require courses in automated integrated production: CIM, CAM , CAD, CNC, and robotics. Engineering Technology degrees have a co-op requirement.

For information, write Northern Kentucky University, Department of Technology, Highland Heights, Kentucky 41706.

Northern Michigan University's department of industrial technologies offers both associate and bachelor's degrees. Course work includes studies in robotics and automation systems, CAD, CAM, flexible manufacturing systems, quality control, and applied programmable controllers. For information, write Department of Industrial Technologies, Northern Michigan University, Marquette, Michigan 49855.

Rensselaer Polytechnic Institute has the Center for Manufacturing Productivity and Technology Transfer (CMP); the Center for Advanced Technology in Robotics and Automation, sponsored by New York State; and the Center for Intelligent Robotic Systems for Space Exploration.

The National Institute of Standards and Technology has named Rensselaer, through the Center for Manufacturing Productivity, as one of five regional manufacturing technology centers in the United States. Major research is being conducted in computer-integrated manufacturing (CIM).

In addition, the program at the Rensselaer Design Research Center focuses on design and engineering modeling, and emphasizes aspects of concurrent engineering.

For information, contact the School of Engineering, Rensselaer Polytechnic Institute, Troy, New York 12180-3590.

Southern College of Technology has two laboratories, each with 25 CAD workstations, and uses them to teach not only CAD, but also the fundamentals of engineering graphics. IBM has contributed hardware, software, and other resources to the college, to aid the school in teaching modern manufacturing methods; the college also has a computer-integrated manufacturing (CIM) lab.

Graduates of the Manufacturing Technology program often take the SME Engineering Fundamentals Exam, offered on campus each year, for SME certification as a certified manufacturing technologist. They may be employed in areas such as steel production and fabrication, aircraft and automobile fabrication and assembly, cable manufacture, and textile mills.

For information, write Southern College of Technology, Mechanical Engineering Technology Department, South Marietta Parkway, Marietta, Georgia 30060.

University of Missouri-Rolla offers a B.S. degree in engineering management. It's based on a three-plus-one formula, in which three years' worth of technical manufacturing engineering course content is blended with a year's worth of technological-managerial course content. The combination synthesizes an effective CIM education that uses CIM laboratory facilities extensively. Also on campus: a CAD and Simulation Laboratory.

For more information, contact Engineering Management Department, University of Missouri-Rolla, Rolla, Missouri 65401.

CHAPTER 9

JOB-HUNTING TIPS

If you want to work in CAD/CAM or related technologies, how do you get your first job in the industry? And, if you already have experience, how can you change jobs profitably? What can you do to improve your chances?

Finding your first job in CAD/CAM may not be as difficult as you'd imagined, particularly if you are proficient in CAD. If you are graduating from a community college or technical institute, you should be working closely with your school placement office to help you arrange job interviews. If you are graduating with an engineering or engineering technology degree, your college or university can often schedule interviews for you with company recruiters who visit the campus. Often, your placement office will critique your resume. Counselors may even videotape you in a mock job interview, analyzing your strengths and weaknesses so you can improve how you come across to potential employers.

There are several strategies you can use to improve your chances, even before you are actively job-hunting for a full-time position. One is to work part-time in CAD while you are going to school or receiving technical training. Major papers in large cities often specify CAD experience as a prerequisite for applicants. Even though you may not yet have worked full-time in CAD, if you can show a prospective employer that you have hands-on experience with a particular CAD package, as well as a desire to succeed in the field, you may be able to negotiate a part-time position as a fill-in, a temporary extra hired to help with a work overload, or a vacation replacement.

Another strategy is to become a co-op student, alternating semesters on campus with time spent on the job. Engineering graduates who've done this have an advantage over those who haven't, say many recruiters. "It's easy to check up on how well such a student has done on the job," says one CAD recruiter. "You can phone their supervisors and get the real low-down on how well they work. You can find out what kinds of hands-on applications students have had. You can learn how a student interacts with different computer systems."

Get involved early in your college years. Join trade associations, especially those with student chapters. Noteworthy are Robotics International, Computer and Automated Systems Association (CASA), and Machine Vision Association of America, all divisions of the Society of Manufacturing Engineers. The Institute of Industrial Engineers is another association you'll want to check out. So is the Society of Women Engineers—which does include members who are men.

SME, IIE, and SWE have professional chapters in major cities. Attending meetings and programs these organizations put on will give you not only a briefing on technology developments, but also an opportunity for professional contacts.

Go to the trade shows, symposiums, and conferences—not only in CAD/CAM, but in related fields, like robotics, machine vision, and other areas of manufacturing technology. You'll find calendars of upcoming events in the trade magazines. For instance, *Managing Automation,* a magazine that covers computer integrated manufacturing heavily, listed 23 such shows in a single issue. Some were primarily regional: for example, Northern California Plant Engineering & Maintenance Show and Material Handling & Packaging Show; and Motion Control Technology Conference & Exhibition/West; others drew audiences from an international base (Autofact Conference and Exposition, for example). *Industrial Engineering,* a magazine that covers systems integration, included listings for a conference on Simulation, an International Conference on Human-Computer Interaction, and the International Conference on Industrial Engineering in its calendar.

Students with appropriate identification who are preregistered can usually attend for substantially less than regular fees.

At the shows, plan to spend time and effort talking to exhibitors, acquiring and studying product literature, and building your own information files. In addition, shows sponsored by associations or other professional groups often have job placement bulletin boards, listing opportunities available to members. Most of these positions require prior previous experience. But even though you may not yet have the skills you need, you'll get an idea of just what is involved in these positions. You may want to broaden your education or experience to round out your qualifications.

CHECK INDUSTRY DEVELOPMENTS

You'll want to research where the jobs are, and how the hiring pattern looks. Read, read, read! You'll need to keep up with business-related publications like *The Wall Street Journal, Fortune,* and *Business Week,* as well as the trades, which regularly cover the job market.

For example, in spring 1993, *Industrial Engineering* reported a survey by the National Association of Manufacturers. Results suggested that manufacturing payrolls would increase just 0.2 percent that year—less than the 1992 increase of 0.3 percent. "The largest manufacturing employment gains in 1993 will be in jobs on the factory floor, while manufacturers hold the line on management and administrative workers," said NAM President Jerry Jasinowski.

You'll want to keep up with developments on trade agreements like the North American Free Trade Agreement (NAFTA). Negotiated and signed during the Bush administration, NAFTA's controversial provisions and potential side agreements will almost certainly impact the numbers of U.S. manufacturing jobs. "The jobs in the U.S. that are vulnerable are not the $6-an-hour jobs, but the $18-an-hour ones, " says Harley Shaiken, labor economist at University of California, San Diego.

Mexico's low-cost labor pool—and hundreds of *maquiladora* (assembly plants located along the U.S.–Mexican border)—have provided attractive opportunities to U.S. manufacturers. Between 1990 and 1993, for instance, General Electric invested $400 million to build refrigerators and ranges in Mexico. Ford and IBM also have Mexican plants, with thousands of employees. *Business Week* reported that productivity grew at twice the U.S. rate between 1988 and 1993. As a result of $26 billion in investment—much of which was spent for new plants and upgrades on existing ones—Mexico created two million new jobs in the five-year period.

Another source of information is *Career Guide to Industries,* published by the U.S. Department of Labor, Bureau of Labor Statistics. You can use this book to check on industries heavily involved with computer-aided design and computer-aided manufacturing.

In September 1992, BLS predicted that employment in the aerospace industry through the year 2005 would remain nearly unchanged, despite the reduction in defense spending. The backlog of orders for the production of commercial aircraft should help protect the industry from economic short-term declines, BLS predicts.

Between 1990–2005, employment in the motor vehicle and equipment industry is expected to decline by 8 percent, or 65,000 jobs, according to BLS. Factory automation should expand, with manufacturers looking to improve productivity through investments in robots, computers, and programmable equipment. That may be good for CAD/CAM jobs, but bad for operators, fabricators, and laborers. Jobs in this industry are highly sensitive to cyclical swings in the economy, and that may affect your prospects.

Although the United States has traditionally been a leader in manufacturing, the move towards a global economy has implications you can't afford to ignore as you plan your strategies for a career in manufacturing automation. For instance, Robert P. Collins, president and CEO of GEFanuc Automation North America, points out that Japan has 176,000 industrial robots, while the U.S. has approximately 33,000. In 1992, a recent survey ranked the U.S. 20th among industrialized nations in per capita consumption of numerically controlled machine tools. Between 1978 and 1989, U.S. exports of finished goods stagnated, Collins says, while imports of finished goods jumped from 66 percent to 77 percent.

While Collins calls for more government investment in advanced production technologies—technologies that presumably include CAD/CAM and robotics—he also predicts a downsizing of industrial organizations. "Industries must also become lean, quality-driven, fast-moving organizations focused on the customer," he suggests.

Does Collins' prediction mean fewer jobs for entering graduates? Maybe. But the U.S. government doesn't necessarily think so. In 1992, the secretaries of Labor and Commerce signed an agreement designed to help companies adopt new production methods. The Labor Department's office of work-based learning was developing a pilot training program that community colleges and others can use to train workers who are new to automated manufacturing technologies.

Other government efforts, begun in 1990, channeled manufacturing outreach efforts through Small Business Development Centers in six states. Maryland, Wisconsin, Pennsylvania, Texas, Missouri, and Oregon matched government funds with state moneys to underwrite small company use of manufacturing databases.

No one can predict with certainty what the job market will be when you are ready to start looking. But as long as you're realistic about your opportunities, as long as you're aggressively pro-active, as long as you work as hard at selling yourself as you have done in acquiring your skills, you've maximized your chances.

READ THE WANT ADS

Check the Sunday papers in your area, looking under various CAD-related headings to see who's hiring. A job advertised in the *Chicago Tribune* called for a CAD/operator and facility planning associate. Successful candidates needed solid VersaCAD 7.0 experience and a college degree with drafting/architectural background and two years' work experience. Lotus 1-2-3 and dBASE IV were pluses. Another architectural office wanted a part-time or full-time person proficient in AutoCAD Release 12.

The engineering department of Imperial Eastman, a manufactuer of refrigeration products, fittings, valves, and specialized hand tools wanted a CAD designer with 3–5 years experience to perform a variety of mechanical design and drafting functions. Two years of technical college were desired, but the company was willing to accept experience and proficiency in CAD as a substitute.

Don't forget to check the *Wall Street Journal National Business Employment Weekly,* a digest of available business positions advertised in the regional editions of the *WSJ*. Though most of the positions are in non-CAD areas, the newspaper runs frequent engineering and technical sections in which CAD-related jobs may be listed. A similar publication is *National Ad Search*. Recent editions of both should be available at your library's reference desk.

CHECK THE TRADES

If you're skilled enough, you may be able to come into CAD from the vendor side. That is, you may be hired to develop software, or to sell it. You'd need excellent programming skills, of course, for the former, and sales skills, as well as a technical background, to be successful in marketing products. Reading the trades regularly will give names and addresses of companies that offer CAD products. For example, *CADalyst Resource and Reference Guide* is published each month in *CADalyst,* a magazine that covers professional management of AutoCAD and related products. The list of hardware and software vendors, characterized by category, includes the name, address, phone number, and (usually) fax number for each. The 12-month compilation is published as *CADalyst Resource and Reference Guide* and issued annually. The 186-page booklet includes a list of user groups, and other reference information.

There's certainly no assurance that any vendor listed is even hiring. However, checking the monthly list or the annual will give you names of companies you might contact in your job search. In addition, joining a users group near you and attending meetings, or going on-line with a user bulletin board, broadens your contacts. *Networking* is an overused phrase, but the concept is effective.

DATABASE JOB POSTINGS

If you have a computer and a modem, you can scan on-line job listings. For example, electronic bulletin boards are offered by the Society of Manufacturing Engineers, and by the U.S. Department of Labor.

To access these (and other) bulletin boards, you'll need to set your communication software to the required parameters: number of data bits, number of stop bits, and parity. Your computer dials up the bulletin board through your modem, makes the connection through an electronic "handshake," and allows you to read the jobs posted.

Call the Society of Manufacturing Engineers in Dearborn, Michigan, to get the bulletin board telephone number (a toll call) and current settings for the board. You'll type in your name, devise and register your own password, and follow the easy on-screen menu prompts.

Typical recent listings on the SME Bulletin Board have included:

- Mechanical Design Engineer. Participate in mechanical engineering design of automotive electronic climate controls; interact with tooling and manufacturing personnel to ensure that product design is compatible with process capabilities; support lead engineer to assure that customer expectations are met; provide support as needed to drafting, modelshop, and manufacturing to resolve issues and problems. Forty hours per week, 8 a.m. to 5 p.m., $36,960. Must have Bachelor of Science degree in mechanical engineering with two courses in mechanical CAD/CAM, one course in computer-aided testing of structures, and one course in vibration analysis.

- Manufacturing Engineer for metalworking company in Northeast Ohio. Implement the manufacturing of CNC high technology-high speed grinding equipment (tool holders and modular tooling systems) using cubic boron nitride (CBN) and vitrified CBN processes. Must be high school graduate, with five years experience. Forty hours per week, 8 a.m. to 5 p.m. Monday–Friday, $39,000 per year.
- Senior production engineering (welding). State-of-the-art southeastern manufacturing company seeks degreed professional with a solid robotic welding portfolio in a concurrent and cellular manufacturing environment.
- Manufacturing Engineer wanted. Computer-aided design of tooling and fixtures for brake housings and carriers. NC programming for Gidding & Lewis machines using CAPT software. Writing programs to be used in a flexible manufacturing system. Using spreadsheets. Using computer-aided-production process plus (CAPP +) software to keep machining time for each component for which has responsibility. Need a Bachelor's degree in Mechanical Engineering and two years experience as a CNC engineer, CAD/CAM engineer, or production engineer.

The electronic bulletin board offered by the U.S. Department of Labor maintains its Federal Job Listings as one of the "Libraries" it offers. By dialing 202-219-4784 (a toll call), and following the on-screen prompts, you'll be able to read up-to-date Federal Job Listings in the Chicago, Atlanta, Philadelphia, Dallas, and San Francisco regions, as well as for the Washington D.C., Atlantic overseas, and Pacific overseas areas. Although most of these jobs aren't CAD/CAM related, occasionally you'll run across one that is.

Other organizations maintain electronic bulletin boards and job listings. When you write to the associations listed in the back of this book in Appendix A, you can ask if they post job openings, and whether or not you must be a member of their particular organization in order to respond.

EMPLOYMENT AGENCIES

Once you have two or three years' experience in factory automation, getting a job related to CAD/CAM or switching companies still isn't easy. The job market in the 1990s is tight; companies may not be hiring, or (understandably) may be promoting from within. Union agreements spelling out seniority may cover who stays and who goes, if layoffs are announced.

Major companies looking for certain training, skills, and experience often use employment agencies. Such agencies frequently advertise in the trade press. Fees for placement come from the *employer*—not from the job candidate. Many states regulate fees and conditions under which agencies doing business in the state must operate.

Most agencies prefer to work with candidates who have from two to five years experience, and who hold four-year degrees. "Typically, I work with the B.S.M.E. (bachelor of science in mechanical engineering) for all mechanical aspects, and the B.S.E.E. (bachelor of science in electrical engineering) for the electronics," says Jim Lakatos, president of IBA Personnel, a Michigan-based employment agency. "All four-year degrees don't carry the same weight with employers, though. I may have a candidate with a 3.9 grade point average on a 4.0 scale who has a four-year B.S. degree in *engineering technology.* Such candidates are more difficult to place than those who have the traditional four-year engineering degree.

"A lot of employers don't like technology degrees. They feel that candidates took the courses because they were easier, or required less math. Now that's not necessarily so. If you're the best designer in a company, it doesn't matter what your degree was. However, if you have a technology degree, it may cost you opportunities when you try to switch companies."

Lakatos doesn't handle first-time-out candidates. Primarily he places candidates with up to five years' experience, at salaries ranging from $30,000 to $42,000. Too much experience with one firm can be a turnoff to potential employers, he says. Lakatos tells of hearing a well-known national recruiter, speaking at a trade seminar, say he won't deal with anyone who's worked more than 6 years with one company. "It's difficult for such a person to leave, to be flexible enough to move to a new employer," the recruiter argued.

One of the most important things for candidates to remember is that their interests and the interests of the employment agency are not necessarily the same. Agencies find people for jobs; they do not find jobs for people. Lakatos reminds candidates that he is looking for a person to fill a corporate vacancy. "The company is paying me," he says. "The candidate isn't."

For a candidate with experience, one of the most important reasons for "signing on" with an agency is the working agreement the agency may have with others in the field. IBA Personnel, the agency Lakatos runs, belongs to a network called Intercity Personnel, based in Wisconsin. "Although the network has professional level openings," he says, "over 90 percent of the placement orders we receive are for engineering candidates.

"If you send me your resume and you're one of my top candidates," he says, "I'll fax it out so that roughly 240 other agencies in my network have your resume." Intercity Personnel is perhaps the third largest network in the U.S., Lakatos explains. Another network has over 400 agencies.

IMPROVING YOUR RESUME

The resume you send an agency or a prospective employer should be the strongest possible. Of course it should look its best, no matter how much time and effort it takes. But you don't have to spend a fortune. Lakatos says having your resume typeset or printed up on fancy paper is a waste of money. White paper, and good-quality typing or good-quality printout, is all you need, he explains. Don't use a dot-matrix printer if you have alternatives; the quality of the letters and type not only doesn't measure up to employers' expectations, but also will not fax well. If you must use a dot-matrix printer, change the ribbon frequently. Even still, typing is better than dot-matrix, Lakatos believes.

Here are some "do's" and "don'ts":

• Make your resume visually attractive.

If you were an employer seeing the resume for the first time, would you want to read it? *Could* you? "I've seen candidates so hung up on getting their resumes on one page that they have 1/4 inch margins, scrunched-together type, and almost no white space," Lakatos says. "I've heard that when a resume hits an employer's desk, it's typically looked at for seventeen seconds the first time around. If it's hard to read or looks cluttered, the resume is usually trashed. You want your resume in the pile put aside to be read later."

Don't go to the other extreme, though. Some candidates send Lakatos resumes more than a dozen pages long; each college gets a separate page, as does each employer. You also don't need to list the courses you've taken.

The ideal length? If you're a just-out-of-school, no-experience candidate, one page. If you have experience, two pages.

And don't use dark-colored paper. It won't fax well. Hold off on the fancy script or elite type, but bold or heavier type is okay to use for key words.

• Do include dates.

Employers want to know when you graduated from college, and when you worked for particular companies. "If you don't include dates," he says, "prospective employers will get the impression you're over 55 with 20 or more years' experience at the same company, probably not flexible enough to move on."

It's okay to say you have gaps in the dates because you've been laid off or dropped in a company reorganization. Just put that information up front in your cover letter, Lakatos advises. Sometimes you may be hired for a company, work only six or seven months, and then be let go. Include the dates, nevertheless.

"If you indicate in your cover letter that you were hired at the time the company was making reductions," he says, "most employers will recognize that you were hired to solve specific problems—you could provide expertise that they didn't have inhouse—and that after you'd solved the problems, you were dropped."

• Include a list with a few of the company's major products when you mention former employers.

Because so many organizations have merged or are part of multinational corporations, a prospective employer may not immediately recognize the names of companies you've worked for. If you say you worked for XYZ Corporation, manufacturer of hydraulic pumps, an employment agency personnel department can tell right away if you have the type of experience that might match their needs. Otherwise, they'll have to check an industrial directory to see what the company makes.

Also, if you worked on a particular product, say so . . . in detail. Were you a machine designer, a control designer, or a project engineer? If you put down that you were, give details.

• Use verbs. Lots of them. Be as specific as possible.

Don't say you participated in the development of a product, even if you did very little as a team member. Instead, say, "I, along with three others, designed a widget." "I designed the simple mechanical aspects of the robotic system." Don't say, "I was involved in—." Instead, tell exactly what you did.

• In your cover letter, indicate that you have transcripts available, references from companies (name them), and a detailed list of projects you've worked on.

Don't include them with the cover letter and resume that go to the employment agency, Lakatos advises. Instead, say you'll be glad to send them on, if wanted. The agency will often request these credentials, and will use them to see how you match up against what its clients (the hiring companies) have in mind.

When you're sending your resume to an employment agency, Lakatos advises, ask what network they belong to. Don't blindly send out a hundred resumes to agencies. Many of them may belong to the same network, and you're just duplicating efforts. "It turns me off a candidate if I find that 33 of his resumes are already in my network," says Lakatos.

If you're not willing to relocate, use a local employment agency. Call for an appointment; take along samples of things you've done: CAD drawings, pictures of machines you've designed, or even a small model. If you're going to look for work on a national basis, contact the employment agencies. Ask upfront if they have people who are working in the geographical locations where you want to be.

PHONE CONTACT IMPORTANT

For candidates who've contacted an agency like Lakatos' by phone, mail, or fax, an important screening comes when an employment counselor calls back. That initial phone contact can make a big difference in the agency's interest.

Most placement counselors do a fast interview over the phone to find out if a candidate whose resume and cover letter sound promising actually meets the guidelines a company has given. A few key questions—and the candidate's response—may determine whether or not the agency is interested in making a match. Says one counselor, "I'll ask you why you want to switch jobs. You'd damn well better tell me you want to make a career move for advancement, or get a better job, or go to a different company in order to further your career.

"If you tell me you want to change jobs to make more money, that's a turnoff. If you're a whiner—if you tell me you don't like your boss—that's a no-no. If you're dissatisfied with your job, be dissatisfied for a concrete reason. Maybe you've reached the limit in what you can do in your present company. That's valid."

Legitimate reasons for job-switching that agencies will usually accept are company mergers or internal consolidation. "I know a company that closed its plant in California, but kept its Michigan operation open," says Lakatos. "In some cases, the jobs were redundant. They didn't need two purchasing managers for the Michigan plant. But the California location had been making a product component, and the Michigan site had to take over. The company needed hydraulic pump designers and project engineering managers in Michigan, but it couldn't just transfer everybody. Some key people refused to leave California. They eventually found new jobs out there, and the company hired appropriate personnel for the Michigan location."

YOUR INTERVIEW WITH THE COMPANY

Occasionally, outstanding candidates may be invited directly to the company's factory or offices for an initial onsite interview. However, the usual next step in screening is a phone interview at a prearranged time with a representative from the manufacturer. The employment agency sets up the interview.

Whenever possible, Lakatos likes to brief "his" candidates before the initial phone interview. He'll fax the candidate the job description, and, when time permits, complete background on the company. Usually the company's initial representative who makes the phone call is a staffer from the human resources department. If candidates still look promising, their names are passed on to the engineering department, who follows up—either by phone, by an invitation to visit the company, or both. "Don't gripe about your former employer," Lakatos says. "Concentrate on presenting your experience. Communication skills help. No one expects you to be a hotshot at sales, but you do have to be able to tell an interviewer exactly what you are doing."

Even if you get the company background from the agency, do your homework. Candidates should be able to discuss companies intelligently. That means library research to find out what the company makes, where it stands in the marketplace, and its organization and financial status. A good place to locate the information is in the company's annual report. You may also want to check *The Wall Street*

Journal index or the *New York Times* index to find out if the company has been mentioned recently.

An interview is a dialogue. You have to show you're really interested. A candidate has to hustle and fight and work hard to get the job. You'll need to ask questions that show you don't want to be stagnant in your career growth.

A HANDS-ON CHALLENGE

Sometimes companies may challenge you unexpectedly to see if you really understand concepts and equipment. Harold Blanthorn, marketing manager of Berhan Industries, Ltd., a CAD service bureau, says an essential part of his company's interviewing is a hands-on test.

"We'll take a CAD drawing that is in progress, or a drawing that may be finished but is going to be changed," he explains. "We'll ask candidates, 'What would you do here?' 'How would you change it there?' If it's at all possible, we'll try to have them sit down at a workstation, mainframe, or PC running AutoCAD. We'll turn the computer on and give them a screen with only a DOS C:> prompt."

Blanthorn says that sometimes candidates have been trained in courses that used machines already configured for AutoCAD; that is, when they turned the computers on and typed *AutoCAD,* the program came up automatically.

"However, in the real world, companies don't all configure computers in the same way," he says. "Persons we hire must already have the basic DOS computer skills. It's nice if they have Windows skills too, but if CAD programs aren't running under Windows, do candidates know what to do?"

Blanthorn says that candidates facing a C:> prompt should know enough to look for a batchfile to call up a CAD program without having to ask for help. (They can do it by typing the DOS command "Dir" at the C:> prompt, looking in the onscreen directory for a file with the extension .EXE, and typing that filename and its .EXE extension.)

CLOSING THE INTERVIEW

"At the end of the interview, or if you're asked what questions you have, show the interviewer that you're interested in improving yourself," advises Lakatos. "Ask if the company has a tuition reimbursement plan. Ask about seminars, conferences, in-service training. Tell the interviewer you want to take courses and gain knowledge that will make you more valuable for the company. In an interview with a company that may hire you, don't ask about retirement benefits or number of weeks of vacation. You can get that information from the human resources department—after you're offered the job."

Even though you want to get into CAD/CAM, and can certainly mention your interest in the technology, don't get hung up during the interview on specific job tasks. "People who say, 'I'll do anything you need; I want to work for your company' get hired a lot quicker than persons who tell the interviewer about what they want to do four years from now," Lakatos warns.

Do write a good, positive follow-up letter, and mail it promptly. If you've met several people onsite, write each individually. Counselors say they've known several candidates who've received job offers because of the quality of their follow-up letters.

RECOMMENDED READING

The following books are especially useful to sharpen your job-hunting skills. There's an additional list of recommended reading in Appendix B.

Bolles, Richard N., *What Color Is Your Parachute?*, Berkeley, California. Ten Speed Press, 1993.

Krannich, Ronald, *High Impact Resumes and Letters*, Manassas Park, Virginia. Impact Publications, 1992.

————. *Interview for Success*, Manassas Park, Virginia. Impact Publications, 1993.

————. *Job Search Letters that Get Results,* Manassas Park, Virginia. Impact Publications, 1992.

Lathrop, Richard, *Who's Hiring Who?,* 12th ed., Berkeley, California. Ten Speed Press, 1989.

Morin, William, *Parting Company: How to Survive the Loss of a Job, and Find Another Successfully,* San Diego, California. Harcourt Brace Jovanovich, 1991.

Parker, Yana, *The Damn Good Resume Guide,* Berkeley, California. Ten Speed Press, 1989.

Peterson's Guides, *The Hidden Job Market: A Job Seeker's Guide to America's 2,000 Little Known, Fastest Growing High-Tech Companies,* Princeton, New Jersey. Peterson, 1991.

Templeton, Mary Ellen, *Help! My Job Interview Is Tomorrow,* New York. Neal-Schuman Publications, 1991.

Wilson, Robert, *Better Resumes for Executives and Professionals,* Hauppauge, New York. Barron, 1991.

CHAPTER 10

OPPORTUNITIES FOR WOMEN
AND MINORITIES

"I never thought that I'd be running a company bigger than the town I grew up in," says Carol Bartz. "I'm from Alma, Wisconsin, a town with 1,000 people. As the CEO of Autodesk, I manage over 1,600 employees."

President, chairman of the board, and CEO of Autodesk, Inc. since 1992, Bartz runs the industry's sixth-largest PC software company . . . the worldwide leader in desktop computer-aided design automation software. The story she told as the Distinguished Alumna of the Year at the University of Wisconsin is an inspiring answer to the question, "Can women succeed in CAD/CAM?"

"As you probably know," says Bartz, "women had limited choices when it came to careers in 1966. Actually, they had two choices. Teaching and nursing. Let's just say I didn't have the patience to be a teacher, and I look terrible in white. I thought of computer science as an unknown, with intriguing potential."

Graduating with honors in computer science, she worked at 3M in St. Paul, Minnesota. She wanted to get involved with marketing . . . to learn how to best position and present a product and ultimately meet customer needs. But she was told that the company would never let a woman into marketing.

"When you're faced with a mountain," she says today, "sometimes the best thing to do is find a valley and go around. A lot of women today feel like they have to climb every mountain. But I say, pick your

104

mountain, because there are a lot of them out there, and you need your energy."

She moved to Digital Equipment Corporation, the company that defined the minicomputer, holding product line and sales management positions. Seven years later, she joined Sun Microsystems as a customer marketing manager. "It's important to broaden your base of experience," she says, "so that as you move up, you have a stable foundation to draw from."

At the time, the company's revenues were $9 million. Within eight months, she replaced the vice president of worldwide marketing, playing a key role in establishing Sun as an open systems vendor. By 1987 she had taken over the company's federal government division. Under her leadership, revenues grew from $21 million to $124 million in just two years.

"At Sun, I was known as a turnaround specialist," she remembers. "I would take the problem-solving skills I had learned, and apply them to new situations." Vice president of customer service, she later became vice president of worldwide field operations. "I rose from $9 million to $3.6 billion, and from 100 to 13,000 employees," she says.

"But then the phone rang. Autodesk was looking for a CEO. Everyone in the industry accepted AutoCAD as the worldwide standard for computer-aided design. And the company was still growing."

In her first year at Autodesk, she convinced the company to broaden its horizons, to feature a family of computer-aided design products to meet customer needs each step along the design process. Along the way, she divested the company's interests in two other unrelated technologies, acquired a complementary company to augment Autodesk's core technology, and internally reorganized the company along vertical markets. "And I grew the company to $350 million in revenues," she says.

THE PATH TO SUCCESS: EDUCATION

Profiled in publications from *Reader's Digest* and *Working Woman* to *Fortune* and *The New York Times,* Carol Bartz is unquestionably the most successful woman in CAD/CAM. But women and members of minority groups who want a career in CAD/CAM or related technologies can also succeed—if they're qualified and willing to work hard, and to be prepared.

Unfortunately, many young women do not realize that substantial numbers of higher-paying jobs require a more quantitative educational background. They pass up science and math courses early in life, thus inadvertently closing the doors on many financially rewarding and enjoyable jobs they might like to hold.

EARLY CHOICES

Based on a Rockefeller Foundation study by Sue E. Berryman, entitled "Who Will Do Science?" the Committee on the Status of Women of the American Physical Society has reported some disturbing conclusions. They've reported two major decision points about women: points where choices must be made about future educational investment.

The first decision point comes much earlier than most students realize. By ninth grade, over one-third of those who will later earn a bachelor's degree in quantitative fields (math, physical or biological sciences, computer science, engineering, and economics) already expect to be scientists. By the end of twelfth grade, the pool is fully established—that is, essentially all those who will go on to a bachelor's degree in quantitative science have already decided to do so.

To succeed in any of these technical fields, and to work in CAD/CAM and related technologies, you'll find that a strong math background helps. Yet one-third fewer females than males choose to take advanced high school math.

Young women, then, are skipping courses that could lead them to well-paying and challenging science careers—including careers in

CAD/CAM, computer science, robotics, and related fields. In particular, they are turning off early on the math they need to succeed.

THE AAUW STUDY

A highly publicized study released in 1991 adds further information about why high school girls may tend to drop math courses earlier in their studies than young men do. The study, commissioned by the American Association of University Women (AAUW), was designed to examine the interaction of self-esteem and education and career aspirations in adolescent girls and boys. Among other topics, the survey examined the relationship of math and science skills to the self-esteem and career goals of the boys and girls in the study.

One of its most significant findings: how students come to regard math and science differs by gender. "Math and science have the strongest relationship on self-esteem for young women," the study says, "and as they 'learn' that they are not good at these topics, their sense of self-worth and aspirations for themselves deteriorate."

The survey found that at all grade levels, adolescent boys are much more confident than young girls about their abilities in math. By high school, one in four males—but only one in seven females—say they are good in math. The study concludes that girls interpret their problems with math as personal failures, while boys project their problems with math more as a problem with the subject matter itself.

A second AAUW Report, "How Schools Shortchange Girls," researched by The Wellesley College Center for Research on Women, is a study of major findings on girls and education. Its findings: "girls are systematically discouraged from courses of study essential to their future employability and economic well-being." By the year 2000, the U.S. work force will require strengths and skills in science, mathematics, and technology—subjects, the report says, that girls are still being told are not suitable for them.

Copies of these, and other AAUW publications, are available for purchase from the American Association of University Women, Sales Office, PO Box 251, 9050 Junction Drive, Annapolis Junction, MD 20701-0251.

SOCIETY OF WOMEN ENGINEERS

For more than 40 years, the Society of Women Engineers (SWE) has actively encouraged women to pursue and excel in engineering careers. The number of women in engineering, although still small, has increased over the years to the point that the Society has over 5,000 professional members and 10,000 student members.

However, since 1987, fewer women have been entering engineering degree programs. In 1992, women made up only 15 percent of the engineers who entered the work force—and only 4 percent of all practicing engineers. The figures are even lower for minorities. As a result, SWE is actively developing outreach programs to encourage minorities to enter science and engineering. In 1989, African Americans and Hispanics each made up less than five percent of those earning bachelor's degrees in engineering; Asian Americans made up just under 10 percent.

THE SWE SCHOLARSHIP PROGRAM

As part of its national educational activities, SWE administers approximately 40 scholarships, totaling more than $60,000 and varying in amount from $1,000 to $4,000. All SWE-administered scholarships are open only to women majoring in engineering in a school, college, or university with an accredited engineering program. They must be in a specified year of study during the academic year after the grant has been presented.

SWE has two National Scholarship Programs. Applications for freshman scholarships and reentry scholarships are available from March through May. Completed applications, including all supporting materials, must be postmarked no later than May 15.

SWE also has a number of scholarships to sophomore, junior, senior, and graduate engineering students. Applications for these scholarships are available from October through January only. Completed applications, including all supporting materials, must be postmarked no later than February 1. Deadline dates for applying for these scholarships are extremely important, warns SWE. Applications postmarked after the submission dates are not considered.

For further information, and to receive scholarship applications, send a self-addressed, stamped envelope to The Society of Women Engineers, United Engineering Center, Room 305, 345 East 47th St., New York NY 10017.

As part of the application, you'll be required to submit transcripts, letters of reference, and an essay on the reasons you've decided to study engineering, why you have chosen your major, and why you are applying for a scholarship.

MINORITY RECRUITMENT

Many engineering schools and companies recruit hard for qualified candidates. Sometimes the recruitment even starts before high school. A nationwide mathematics coaching and competition program, aimed at combating math illiteracy, is open to seventh- and eighth-graders; for information, contact the National Society of Professional Engineers (NSPE), Information Center, 1420 King St., Alexandria, VA 22314.

Most engineering colleges and universities have special programs for culturally disadvantaged students. Minority students often take advantage of these programs. One program which has received nationwide recognition is Georgia Tech's freshman engineering workshop, which invites ninth-grade students from minority backgrounds to visit the campus, meet with faculty, visit companies that employ engineers, and plan careers in engineering or related fields. For additional information on this program, write Director of Special Programs, College of Engineering, Georgia Institute of Technology, Atlanta, GA 30332.

Similar enrichment, awareness, or recruitment programs often exist at universities in metropolitan areas. Illinois Institute of Technology has summer programs for talented, minority, Chicago-area high school juniors interested in math, science, or engineering. Some scholarships are available. Write to the Illinois Institute of Technology, Engineering Department, 3300 South Federal Av., Chicago, IL 60616.

At the University of Texas-Austin, the Equal Opportunities in Engineering Program includes scholarships. Write to the University of Texas-Austin, Equal Opportunities in Engineering, College of Engineering, ECJ2-102, Austin, TX 78712.

To locate such programs, ask your school guidance counselor for details, or write to an affirmative action officer at a college or university near you.

Another excellent source of information is *MEPS/USA: The Directory of Precollege and University Minority Engineering Programs.* Available for purchase and inexpensive, the directory covers more than 50 precollege and university engineering programs for minority students, geographically arranged. It's published in July of even years. For information, write the National Action Council for Minorities in Engineering (NACME), Three W. 35th St., New York, NY 10001.

NACME says the number of underrepresented minority students earning degrees in engineering hit an all-time high of 4,681 in 1992— approximately 7.4 percent of the graduating class. Increases were noted for African Americans, Hispanics, and Native Americans. However, the number of minority women dropped slightly. The number of African-American women stayed constant; Hispanic women declined slightly; and Native American women increased from 27 to 32.

ENGINEERING PUBLICATIONS

You'll find *Minority Engineer* an exceptionally valuable publication. The magazine is one in a series of technically oriented publications that offer role-model profiles and career-guidance strategies that reflect the changing diversified work force.

By the year 2000, 65 percent of the work force will consist of members of minority groups, women, and people with disabilities, points out John R. Miller III, president of Equal Opportunity Publications, which publishes the magazines. The company also has published a *Workforce Diversity Journal* as a permanent reference guide for companies and associations serving minority engineers.

The spring 1993 issue of *Minority Engineer* featured a cover story on Alfonso Bonilla, a senior industrial engineer/Computer Integrated Manufacturing (CIM) project leader at Ethicon, a Johnson & Johnson company. Helping to develop what he terms "the manufacturing plant of the future," Bonilla says that CIM, combined with streamlined manufacturing processes, will help Johnson & Johnson produce better quality products at lower cost. A 1982 industrial engineering graduate of the State University of Buffalo, he says internship can provide the necessary tie-in between academics and job experience.

Bonilla, who credits Johnson & Johnson with commitment to managing diversity, has served as a member of the action team that identifies issues that tend to be barriers for women and people of color. However, he told *Minority Engineering,* "If you work aggressively, take risks, and work hard to accomplish realistic goals, barriers can definitely be broken."

Editor Jim Schneider recommends several of Equal Opportunity Publications' other magazines: *Equal Opportunity, Woman Engineer* (which the Society of Women Engineers helps to distribute), and *Career Woman,* the only woman's magazine that deals exclusively with careers at the entry level. *CAREERS & the disABLED* has been cited by the President's Committee on Employment of People with Disabilities and the Library of Congress as contributing to the employment of people with disabilities.

Included in each of the recruitment magazines are resume referral and corporate listing of employer advertisers.

If you are a minority engineering college graduate (or within two years of graduating) or a minority professional engineer, you can receive *Minority Engineer* free. A similar arrangement exists for *Woman Engineer.* Otherwise, you can pick up a sample copy at your college career guidance office, or write for information to Circulation Department, Equal Opportunity Publications, Inc., 150 Motor Parkway, Suite 420, Hauppauge, New York 11788-5145.

SPECIAL HELP

A number of organizations provide help, guidance, materials, and even scholarships to women and minority students who want to be engineers. While they aren't necessarily focused on CAD/CAM and related technology, nevertheless they're worth looking into.

Films about engineering your teacher can order directly and show in class include:

Bridging New Worlds (Uniendo Nuevos Mundos), a film in English with Spanish subtitles, helps parents and encourages their children to study engineering and the applied sciences. For information, contact Bilingual Cine Television, 2601 Mission Street, Suite 703, San Francisco, CA 94110.

Technology Occupations (order #VT-02) is a videotape for junior and senior high students that highlights careers in drafting, plastics, computer sciences, electrical technology, programming, and tool building. *Engineering Disciplines* (order #VT-01), also for junior and senior high students, highlights careers in structural, electrical, manufacturing, aeronautical, mechanical, and chemical engineering. Information on ordering these videos is available from JETS, the Junior Engineering Technical Society, 1420 King St., Suite 405, Alexandria, VA 22314-2715. JETS also has career literature available.

JETS can also give you information on the National Engineering Aptitude Search. While the exam is not specifically aimed at women and minorities, it serves as a guidance-oriented test for high school students who are considering careers in engineering, math, science, or technology, and helps determine students' strengths and weaknesses.

SOUTHEASTERN CONSORTIUM FOR MINORITIES

For nearly 20 years, the Southeastern Consortium for Minorities in Engineering (SECME), has helped increase the number of minorities studying and earning degrees in engineering, mathematics, and science. SECME students compete for industry and university scholarships.

The organization works directly with high schools and teachers. Its programs help middle grade teachers to meet the needs of minority students and keep those students interested in math and science by "doing." SECME's cross-cultural workshops show teachers how to understand and value cultural differences in the classroom, making teachers sensitive to students' needs, customs, traditions, and learning styles. Teachers learn how to help students work effectively as a team with classmates from different cultural backgrounds.

SECME's Summer Institute includes an annual student competition among high school finalists from the local and state levels. For information, write to the Southeastern Consortium for Minorities in Engineering (SECME), Georgia Institute of Technology, Atlanta, GA 30332-0270.

NATIONAL SOCIETY OF BLACK ENGINEERS

Another organization you'll find helpful is the National Society of Black Engineers (NSBE). Through national and regional conferences, NSBE encourages and advises disadvantaged young people to pursue engineering careers. A career fair, resume books, and technical seminars are part of the annual national conference.

Members of this student-run, nonprofit organization visit schools and host junior and high school students on campuses. NSBE presents scholarships to high school seniors and, with support from the corporate sector, NSBE presents scholarships based on scholastic achievement.

For information, write the National Society of Black Engineers (NSBE), 344 Commerce St., Alexandria VA 22314.

OTHER ORGANIZATIONS

If you're a minority student, especially if you're studying engineering or engineering-related courses, you'll want to take advantage of all the help that's available. Often this includes summer programs before the freshman year of college, developmental year programs, which have special courses, and tutoring. Taking part in programs like this is time well spent; make a special effort to look for help and take advantage of opportunities.

You'll want to look for student chapters of national associations on your campus, or for senior chapters nearby. Join them and attend meetings. Organizations such as the Society of Manufacturing Engineers (SME), the Institute of Industrial Engineers, and the Society of Women Engineers all have extremely active chapters. In fact, the Society of Women Engineers had roughly 9,000 student members in 1992. Taking an active, leadership role in organizations like these can not only give you valuable experience, but can also help you make contacts that can be helpful as you enter the job market.

SPECIAL PUBLICATIONS

A new series of ethnic titles, often on reference shelves at public and college libraries, has extremely useful information. Available from Gale Research Inc., and updated periodically, the series includes:

- *Asian Americans Information Directory*
- *Black Americans Information Directory*
- *Hispanic Americans Information Director*
- *Native Americans Information Directory*

Typical of the books in the series, *Hispanic Americans Information Directory,* a biennial book published in October of odd years, is a guide to approximately 4,700 organizations, agencies, institutions, programs, and publications concerned with Hispanic American Life and Culture. Included are listings of associations; awards, honors, and prizes; bilingual and migrant education programs; the top 500 businesses; cultural organizations; government agencies and programs; libraries; newspapers and periodicals; research centers; and videos.

Organizations and publications are described in detail. For instance, the *Society of Hispanic Professional Engineers—National Newsletter* describes reports on activities, programs, and workshops of the Association; announcements of educational and job opportunities and scholarships; affiliate association and member news; calendar of events; and columns.

Here are several additional organizations that specifically target minorities and offer career information:

Hispanic Society of Engineers and Scientists (HSES)
P.O. Box 1393
Richland, WA 99352

Mexican-American Engineering Society (MAES)
P.O. Box 3520
Fullerton, CA 92634

Mid-America Consortium for Scientific and Engineering
Achievement
c/o Engineering Department
Durland Hall, Kansas State University
Manhattan, KS 66506

Mid-American Chinese Science and Technology Association
(MACSTA)
P.O. Box 4528
Naperville, IL 60567

National Action Council for Minorities in Engineering (NACME)
3 West 35th St.
New York, NY 10001

National Council of La Raza (NCLR)
955 L'Enfant Plaza SW, Suite 4000
Washington, DC 20024

Society for the Advancement of Chicanos and Native Americans
    in Science (SACNAS)
    P.O. Box 30030
    Bethesda, MD 20814

Society of Spanish Engineers, Planners & Architects
    P.O. Box 75
    Church Street Station
    New York, NY 10007

GETTING HIRED

If you've successfully completed your schooling, especially if you have an engineering degree, finding a job in CAD/CAM will be *easier* than average, several college placement officers say. For the past five years, the top student in Rutgers University's Industrial Engineering program has been a woman; the 1993 graduate had five job offers and accepted a position with a starting salary of nearly $40,000.

Jim Schneider, editor of *Minority Engineering,* says that one reason your chances are excellent is that any firms using CAD and CAM, especially in aerospace and defense work, receive government contracts. When they do, Schneider says, they're required to hire a certain percentage of underrepresented groups. Consequently, women and minorities have a good opportunity in engineering, where they might not have such chances in other fields.

Here's how Autodesk's CEO Carol Bartz sees your chances: "Yes, you can take intelligent risks, jump completely out of your element, and even make a lateral move in order to gain experience and skills. The more prepared you are, the better you will be able to understand and help employees, coworkers, and bosses be better team players and succeed. The more prepared you are, the better you will be able to lead."

CHAPTER 11

INTERNATIONAL OPPORTUNITIES

Many experts talk about the global market for products and services. Certainly, major companies, especially those in manufacturing, have already shifted production facilities overseas to take advantage of lower labor costs. Many companies are multinational—part of conglomerates controlled by investors from outside the United States. In addition, U.S.-based companies are entering into production agreements with factories in other countries. In short, high technology such as CAD/CAM and robotics is by no means limited to one or two countries.

Today, technology is moving quickly, and the rate at which it's changing is faster than ever. In addition, political and economic developments have transformed traditional alliances. Consequently, your chances of finding a job in CAD or CAM in countries outside the United States are going to depend not only on your technical competency, but also on factors very much beyond your control.

For instance, the phaseout of Section 936 of the Internal Revenue Code, which allowed U.S. corporations to escape federal corporate taxes on products made in Puerto Rico, may well cause factories there to be shut down in favor of Ireland or Singapore—two locations where taxes are lower. *Business Week* predicts the phaseout will jeopardize many of Puerto Rico's 152,000 manufacturing jobs. Until the 1993 Congressional vote on the phaseout, manufacturing had accounted for 40 percent of Puerto Rico's gross domestic product.

The North American Free Trade Agreement (NAFTA), a controversial plan to let goods and services move more freely among the United States, Canada, and Mexico, will certainly impact jobs in manufacturing.

MARKETPLACE GROWTH

Slow economic growth, coupled with an extremely competitive marketplace, have cut potential jobs in Europe. The unification of Germany and the consolidation of the European Community (EC) have already begun to impact on manufacturing there—in particular, steel, auto, machine tooling, and other heavy industry. Yet jobs in factory automation—the CAM side of CAD/CAM—may be a necessary part of Europe's catchup strategy.

The Economist Intelligence Unit, a New York- and London-based research firm that tracks business developments, reported in 1993 that the Japanese had left European vehicle assembly plants far behind in advanced automation, flexibility, and productivity. EIU says Japan's manufacturers take 16–18 hours to assemble a car, versus European manufacturers' 26–28 hours. A Japanese worker puts out 48 cars a year; a European worker, 22 to 34 cars.

Concurrent engineering for new products has cut time for new model development. The Japanese take 28 to 30 months; Volkswagen, using concurrent engineering technology, still takes 32 to 36 months to develop new model cars.

SOFTWARE

Possibly as a consequence, manufacturing software—systems that handle CAD/CAM, manufacturing execution, and factory data collection—is on the upswing. Market Intelligence Research Corp., which tracks such information and produces reports for sale, says users were buying $6.3 billion worth of the software in 1993, versus $3.1 billion in 1992. The corporation makes its projections because of the trend toward open systems that can make software run on many computer hardware platforms.

Tying systems together in networks—electronic data information exchange—may also be an area in which jobs will expand. *Fortune* predicts that "corporations will be linked into increasingly coherent networks that connect all varieties of computers—from big iron to laptops to the pocket devices of tomorrow. The servers—a term for the computers that hold the information, much as a library has collections of books—will act as central repositories of data, holding anything from corporate files to videos and voice-mail messages."

At $360 billion a year, computing is one of the largest industries in the world. CAD/CAM and related technologies are a small part of that industry. But for you, they may be your career—in Singapore, in Taiwan, in Brazil, as well as in Canada, Australia, and the UK.

There are tremendous opportunities worldwide in CAD/CAM. The only limit is your imagination!

ASSOCIATIONS

While there are no associations that deal solely with CAD, and just one that deals solely with CAM, the trade associations listed below are excellent sources of information on these (and related) technologies. Several have student chapters. In addition, some of the associations have chapters in major cities. You can almost always attend meetings if you pay a small guest fee. SME and IIE meetings often feature plant tours; visiting factories as part of a group like this is an excellent way to learn about advances in technology. You'll find additional associations listed in Chapter 10 of this book, "Opportunities for Women and Minorities." Check them out; they have excellent publications, and they're valuable sources of information.

American Design Drafting Association
    5522 Norbeck Rd., Suite 391
    Rockville, MD 20853

American Institute of Architects
    1735 New York Ave. NW
    Washington, DC 20006

Computer-Aided Manufacturing International
    1250 E. Copeland Rd., No. 500
    Arlington, TX 76011

Industrial Designer Society of America
  1142 E. Walker Rd.
  Great Falls, VA 22066

Institute of Industrial Engineers (IIE)
  25 Technology Park/Atlanta
  Norcross, GA 30092

Society of Manufacturing Engineers (SME)
  One SME Drive
  Dearborn, MI 48121

Society of Women Engineers (SWE)
  Room 305
  345 E. 47th St.
  New York, NY 10017

RECOMMENDED READINGS AND RESOURCES

PERIODICALS

If you want to work in CAD or CAM, or in related technologies, start now to learn all you can about this rapidly changing field. You can benefit greatly from keeping abreast of this complex technology—not only in architectural and design developments, but also in manufacturing. In addition, you'll want to monitor developments in the broader issues that factory automation raises by reading such periodicals as *Fortune, Business Week,* and (to a lesser extent) *U.S. News & World Report.*

You can start locating information by looking up the appropriate subjects in *Ulrich's International Periodicals Directory,* a book you'll almost certainly find at the reference desk of your school or public library. Also, if you're interested in CAD as part of architecture, a list of accredited programs in architecture, and professional degrees conferred on completion of their curricula in architecture, is available from the National Architectural Accrediting Board, Inc., 1735 New York Ave. NW, Washington, DC 20006.

Periodicals in the field of manufacturing engineering, including those magazines and reports that concentrate on news about factory automation, continue to discuss such topics as cost justification, retraining workers in skills needed for new technology in factory automation, and retrofitting existing plants. Of course, new products and new applications of existing products are covered. Periodicals also report on the economics of manufacturing, as well as on what major companies are doing that has an impact on jobs and products.

Keeping up with industry developments by reading several periodicals regularly is a good idea. You'll be able to assess what is happening, and how these developments can directly affect you.

How to Keep Up

There are several ways to keep up with the literature. One resource available in a growing number of public libraries is "InfoTrac," an easy-to-use online database that indexes recent magazines. Its "general business" version asks you to type in your desired subject. Then you'll move cursor keys around to highlight articles that interest you. Often, a short abstract, usually under 10 lines long, is listed under the article's title. You can print out all the references and look them up later.

A second good way is to check your public or university library for *Applied Science and Technology Index* and the *Business Periodicals Index*. These specialized indexes are put out by the same company that issues the familiar *Readers' Guide to Periodical Literature*. They're updated monthly, with three months' worth of citations grouped together in quarterly paperback volumes. Eventually, all the updates are combined in an annual volume. Both indexes are cross-referenced, so that if you look for the topic *Computer-Aided Design,* you will be referred to articles on related topics. If it seems as if these topics overlap, they do. You may find the same citation under several different headings.

For ease in using the indexes, you may want to photocopy the pages listing the citations. Then you can take them home and review them, deciding on what you really want most to read. You can also ask your reference librarian for a list of what publications the particular library you are using subscribes to, and whether nearby libraries have some of the others. A comparison of the lists will show you quickly whether the articles which interest you are easily obtainable.

It is highly unlikely that the average public library will subscribe to all these specialized journals and trade publications. However, many libraries belong to services which can obtain copies of individual articles—often at no charge or for an extremely inexpensive fee. There are copyright rules which the library may use as guidelines to limit the number of articles from any particular journal or issue.

In the front of *Applied Science and Technology Index* and *Business Periodicals Index,* you will find a list of the periodicals covered by that particular index, along with the address of the magazine. Costs of a subscription are listed in *The Gale Directory of Publications and Broadcast Media,* which is updated yearly and available at the reference desk of your library. Costs usually are listed for a sample copy, so that you can write to the publisher directly and enclose your check or money order.

If you are asking a publisher outside your own country to send you a sample copy, talk with your post office or postal authority about buying international money orders and international postal reply coupons. Publishers abroad may be reluctant to accept personal checks. Also, sending them the international postal reply coupons (which you buy at your local post office) lets them exchange the coupons for postage in their own country's stamps. Don't forget to let the publisher know whether you want the sample sent by surface mail or by air. If it's to come by air, be sure to enclose enough international postal reply coupons to cover the cost of airmail postage, and say so explicitly in your letter.

Automotive Industries
  1 Chilton Way
  Radnor PA 19089-0030
Articles on key industry personnel, automotive manufacturing, and the design/build process cover U.S. and international news. A typical article on CAD/CAM, from a recent issue, described a solid modeling system that assembles as it builds in a new approach to rapid prototyping, using a CAD data file.

Automotive Engineering
  c/o Society of Automotive Engineers
  400 Commonwealth Dr.
  Warrendale PA 15096

Articles, photos, and drawings about advances in technology in the auto industry. The magazine monitors government action, including developments in technology that strengthen U.S. industry's competitiveness.

Aviation Week & Space Technology
  Suite 1200—1120 Vermont Ave. NW
  Washington DC 20005

Nine articles on CAD/CAM/CAE published in 1992 indicate the depth of this publication's coverage. Articles included stories on CAD software packages, and user applications by Boeing and McDonnell Douglas.

Canadian Architect
  Southam Business Communications, Inc.
  1450 Don Mills Rd.
  Don Mills Ontario M3B 2X7
  Canada

Careers in Aerospace
  American Institute of Aeronautics & Astronautics
  370 L'Enfant Promenade SW
  Washington DC 20024-2518

More a guidance booklet than a true periodical, this 18-page publication describes a typical curriculum, discusses where the industry is going, and lists colleges and universities with AIAA student branches. Modest scholarships are also available to student members enrolled as undergraduate students at accredited colleges or universities.

CE Computing Review
  American Society of Civil Engineers
  345 E. 47th St.
  New York NY 10017-2398

The computing newsletter for civil engineers occasionally runs an issue devoted to CAD. Editor Lisa Beckman suggests, however, that students will be better off getting a full engineering degree rather than concentrating only on CAD/CAM. "Computer-aided engineering design is enormously complicated," she says. "It requires sound engineering experience to avoid costly and sometimes deadly mistakes."

COAL
Maclean Hunter Publishing Co.
29 N. Wacker Dr.
Chicago IL 60606-3298

COAL magazine, a technical trade publication geared toward professionals in the coal industry, provides up-to-date news about new technologies, procedures, and policies that affect the coal industry. Most readers are mining engineers who work in all phases of mine management and production. Technical editor Steve Fiscor says the coal industry offers a lot of opportunities for people with CAD training—especially in digitizing mine maps. On the supply side, he says, CAM comes into play with specialized machine-shop fabrication.

The CAD Rating Guide
Zem Press
8220 Stone Trail Dr.
Bethesda MD 20817-4556

The third edition (1993) is available both in paper and as a computer disk database. Editor Brad Holtz says the package is used by CAD vendors and users, by people who don't yet have CAD systems and want to buy them, and by prospective CAD software customers who plan to work with more than one CAD system.

Computer Aided Design Report (The *CAD Report*)
Suite D
841 Turquoise St.
San Diego CA 92109

Monthly newsletter that summarizes significant advances in CAD/CAM technology, reviews important trends in CAD/CAM, and describes how innovative companies are using the technology to boost productivity and save money.

Also from the same company: *Rapid Prototyping Report, CAD/CAM Strategic Planning Guide, The Smart Manager's Guide to Effective CAD Management, Product Data Management Buyer's Guide.*

Computer Design
Penwell Publishing Co.
1421 S. Sheridan
PO Box 1260
Tulsa OK 74101

Designfax
Huebcore Communications, Inc.
1355 Mendota Heights Rd., Suite 210
Mendota Heights MN 55120
Professional design engineers stay current with this useful, practical, easy-to-read source on changing technologies and new products. You'll find information on product design trends and new design technology in electrical and electronic design, fluid power, materials, mechanical components, CAD, computer, and other engineering-related devices and equipment.

Similar publications from the same company include *Metalfax* (metalcutting, metalforming, fabrication, quality, and automation), and *Medical Equipment Designer.* Only qualified professionals receive these controlled circulation publications, but sample copies are available from the publisher on request.

Design Methods and Theories
Design Methods Institute
Box 5
San Luis Obispo CA 93406

Design News
Cahners Publishing Co.
8773 S. Ridgeline Blvd.
Highlands Ranch CO 80126
This magazine blends articles with primarily technical vocabulary with easy-to-read illustrated features on industrial topics. Its audience

is primarily design engineers. New product information and technology business briefs are included for a variety of industries.

Electronic Design
611 Route 46 West
Hasbrouck Heights NJ 07604

A worldwide audience of engineers and engineering managers uses this fairly technical magazine to keep up with developments in processor chips, power op amps, flash converters, and other such subjects.

Engineering Digest
Canadian Engineering Publications Ltd.
5080 Timerlea Blvd. - Ste. 8
Mississauga Ontario L4W 5Cl
Canada

Canada and UK news of interest to engineers is highlighted, along with new product descriptions. Each main feature article is summarized in English and in French.

Engineering News-Record (ENR)
McGraw-Hill Information Service Company
1221 Avenue of the Americas
New York NY 10020

Engineering News-Record is a weekly news magazine that covers the broad spectrum of construction in all areas—building, highway, and heavy. Readers are everyone in the construction process—from architect to engineer to designer to developer. The magazine supplies news and information on projects, new technologies, legislation and its impact, as well as cost data.

Guidelines Letter
(new directions and techniques in the design professions)
Box 456
Orinda CA 94563

Heating, Piping, and Air Conditioning
Penton Publishing
1100 Superior Ave.
Cleveland OH 44114-2543

The magazine of mechanical systems engineering, this publication concentrates on news and trends in that field. An occasional article on CAD use appears.

Industrial Engineering
Institute of Industrial Engineers
25 Technology Park/Atlanta
Norcross GA 30092

This publication is concerned with the design, improvement, and installation of integrated systems of people, material, information, equipment, and energy. Many articles on automating production lines are carried—in colorful, easy-to-read form.

Journal of Computing in Civil Engineering
American Society of Civil Engineers
345 E. 47th St.
New York NY 10017-2398

Also publishes: *Journal of Construction Engineering & Management; Journal of Irrigation and Drainage Engineering; Journal of Management in Engineering; Journal of Structural Engineering; Journal of Transportation Engineering.*

Managing Automation
Thomas Publishing Co.
Five Penn Plaza
New York NY 10001

This publication considers itself the magazine of computer integrated manufacturing. Current news of industry developments and companies, an international report on automation, a calendar of events, and a regular section of industry "opinion" from leaders in manufacturing automation integrate technical and business information.

Manufacturing Engineering
Society of Manufacturing Engineers
One SME Dr.
Dearborn MI 48121

The flagship publication of the Society of Manufacturing Engineers, *Manufacturing Engineering* features successful "we did it" stories about companies that use CAD, CAM, and related technologies as part of computer integrated manufacturing.

Mining Engineering
Society for Mining, Metallurgy, & Exploration Inc.
8307 Shaffer Parkway
PO Box 625002
Littleton CO 80127-4102

Plastics Technology
355 Park Ave. South
New York NY 10010-1789
A "technology news" section often includes news about CAD/CAM, and CIM. Also included: information on stereo-lithography and other rapid-prototyping technologies.

Plastics World
Cahners Publishing Co.
Cahners Building
275 Washington St.
Newton MA 02158-1630

P/O/P Times (The National News Publication of Point/of/Purchase Advertising and Display)
2000 N. Racine Ave.
Chicago IL 60614

Robotics World
6151 Powers Ferry Rd. NW
Atlanta GA 30339-2941
This controlled-circulation trade publication goes only to qualified recipients—i.e., people who are currently working in the robotics field and whose job titles match the target audience.

Each issue includes product application articles. An annual Robotics World directory lists robot manufacturers/robotic/vision systems integrators, suppliers' applications, robotic research, consultants, and training programs. The magazine is available in libraries which maintain a paid subscription.

Technology Review
Building W-59
201 Vassar St.
Cambridge MA 02139

Tooling & Production
Huebcore Communications Inc.
29100 Aurora Rd. - Suite 200
Cleveland OH 44139

The magazine of manufacturing technology and management, *Tooling & Production* provides in-depth coverage of advances in manufacturing automation and control. Recent articles include "The Promise of Robotics," a look at the future of robots in manufacturing.

BOOKS

You'll want to read books on computer-aided design and computer-aided manufacturing, along with books on robotics, machine vision, CNC machining, and related technologies. The following books and publications are recommended. Read Chapter 8 ("Education and Training") in this book to learn about directories you may want to order. Check *Subject Guide to Books in Print* for additional titles.

Autofact '92, Conference Proceedings, Nov. 10–12, 1992, Detroit MI, Dearborn, MI. SME, 1993.

CADalyst Resource and Reference Guide, Eugene, Oregon. Aster Publishing Corporation, 1992.

Computer Aided Design Report, monthly newsletter, San Diego, California. CAD/CAM Publishing, Inc.

Fifth International Service Robot Congress: Proceedings, Ann Arbor, Michigan. Robotic Industries Association, 1988.

International Robot & Vision Automation Conference Proceedings, Ann Arbor, Michigan. Robotic Industries Association, 1991.

MVA/SME Machine Vision Industry Directory, Dearborn, Michigan. SME, 1991.

RI/SME Robotics Research & Development Lab Directory, Dearborn, Michigan. SME, 1991.

Robotics, rev. ed. (Understanding Computers Set), Alexandria, Virginia. Time-Life, 1991.

Vision '90 Conference Proceedings, held Nov. 12–15, 1990, Detroit, Michigan. Dearborn, Michigan. Society of Manufacturing Engineers, 1990.

Asfahl, C. Ray, *Robots and Manufacturing Automation,* New York. John Wiley & Sons, Inc., 1992.

Bertain, Leonard, ed., *CIM Implementation Guide,* 3rd ed., Dearborn, MI. SME, 1991.

Bolhouse, Valerie, *Fundamentals of Machine Vision,* Dearborn, Michigan. (self-published), 1991.

Bone, Jan, *Opportunities in Robotics Careers,* 2nd ed., Lincolnwood, Ill., VGM Career Horizons, 1993.

Boothroyd, G., *Assembly Automation and Product Design,* New York. Marcel Dekker, 1992.

Bresticker, R., *American Manufacturing and Logistics in the Year 2001,* Hoffman Estates, IL. Brigadoon Bay Books, 1992.

Chang, Tien-Chien, et al, *Computer-Aided Manufacturing,* New York. Prentice-Hall, 1990.

Choi, B.K., *Surface Modeling for CAD-CAM: Advances in Industrial Engineering, Ser.: No 11,* Madison Square Station, NY. Elsevier, 1991.

Crosley, Mark Lauden, *The Architect's Guide to Computer-Aided Design,* New York. John Wiley & Sons, 1988.

Dorf, Richard and, Nof, Shimon Y., eds., *Concise International Encyclopedia of Robotics,* New York. John Wiley & Sons, Inc., 1990.

Galbiati, L., Jr., *Machine Vision and Digital Image Processing Fundamentals,* New York. Prentice Hall, 1990.

Gibbs, D. and Crandell, T., *An Introduction to CNC Machining and Programming,* New York. Industrial Press, 1991.

Goetsch, David L., *CAD Applications: Architecture,* Albany, NY. Delmar, 1986.

Goetsch, D., *Advanced Manufacturing Technology Book,* Dearborn, Michigan. SME & Delmar, 1990.

Gross, Larry D., *Fundamentals of CAD with CADKEY for Engineering Graphics,* New York. Macmillan, 1990.

Jacobs, Paul F., *Rapid Prototyping & Manufacturing: Fundamentals of StereoLithography,* Dearborn, MI. SME, 1992.

Hall, E. L., et al, eds., *Expert Robots for Industrial Use,* VOL 1008, Boston. SPIE-Society of Photo-Optical Instrumentation Engineers, 1989.

Henderson, T.C., *Traditional & Non-Traditional Robotic Sensors,* New York. Springer-Verlag, 1990.

Hoshizaki, Jon & Bopp, Emily, *Robot Applications Design Manual,* New York. John Wiley & Sons, Inc., 1990.

Hunt, V. Daniel, *Understanding Robotics,* San Diego, California. Academic Press, 1990.

Jarvis, R.A., ed., *Robots: Coming of Age,* New York. Springer-Verlag, 1989.

Lane, J., ed., *Automated Assembly,* 2nd ed., Dearborn, MI. SME, 1986.

Leatham-Jones, B., *Elements of Industrial Robotics,* East Brunswick, New Jersey. Nichols Publishing Co., 1989.

LeMaistre, Christopher and El-Sawy, Ahmed, *Computer Integrated Manufacturing: A Systems Approach,* White Plains, NY. Quality Resources, 1987.

McKerrow, Philip, *Introduction to Robotics,* Redding, Massachusetts. Addison-Wesley, 1991.

Muglia, V.O., ed., *Enterprise Information Exchange: A Roadmap for Electronic Data Interchange for the Manufacturing Company,* Dearborn, MI. SME, 1993.

National Center for Manufacturing Sciences, *Competing in World-Class Manufacturing: America's 21st Century Challenge,* Homewood, Illinois. Dow-Jones Irwin, 1990.

Nolen, J., *Computer-Automated Process Planning for World-Class Manufacturing,* New York. Marcel Dekker Inc., 1989.

Nyman, L., ed., *Making Manufacturing Cells Work,* Dearborn, MI. SME, 1992.

Pingry, J., *Practical Machine Vision,* Arlington, Massachusetts. Cutter Information Corporation, 1987.

Salant, Michael A., *Introduction to Robotics,* New York. McGraw-Hill, Inc., 1988.

Sharon, D., Harstein, J., Yantian, G., *Robotics and Automated Manufacturing,* East Brunswick, New Jersey. Nichols Publishing Co., 1989.

Thacker, R., *A New CIM Model: A Blueprint for the Computer-Integrated Manufacturing Enterprise,* Dearborn, MI. SME, 1989.

Thomas Jr., R. Roosevelt, *Beyond Race and Gender,* New York. Amacom, 1991.

U.S. Department of Labor, Bureau of Labor Statistics, *Career Guide to Industries* (Bulletin 2403), Washington DC, 1992.

U.S. Department of Labor, Bureau of Labor Statistics, *Outlook 1990–2005* (Bulletin 2402), Washington DC, 1992.

West, Perry, *Machine Vision Lighting and Optics,* Campbell, California. Automated Vision Systems Inc., 1991.

Wysack, Roy, *Smart Manager's Guide to Effective CAD Management,* 2nd ed., San Diego, California. CAD/CAM Publishing, Inc., 1992.

Zuech, N., *Applying Machine Vision,* New York. John Wiley & Sons, 1988.

Zuech, N., ed., *Gaging with Vision Systems,* Dearborn, Michigan. Society of Manufacturing Engineers, 1987.

————. *Machine Vision: Capabilities for Industry,* Dearborn, Michigan. Society of Manufacturing Engineers, 1986.

APPENDIX C

LABOR OFFICES

REGIONAL OFFICES, BUREAU OF APPRENTICESHIP AND TRAINING

Location

Regional Director, Region I
11th floor
One Congress Street
Boston, Massachusetts 02114
States served: Connecticut,
Maine, Massachusetts, New
Hampshire, Rhode Island,
Vermont.

Regional Director, Region II
Room 602—Federal Building
201 Varick Street
New York, New York 10014
Areas served: New Jersey, New
York, Puerto Rico, Virgin Islands.

Regional Director, Region III,
Room 13240—Gateway Building
3535 Market Street
Philadelphia, PA 19104
States served: Delaware,
Maryland, Pennsylvania, Virginia,
West Virginia.

Regional Director, Region IV
Room 418
1371 Peachtree Street, N.E.
Atlanta, Georgia 30367
States served: Alabama, Florida,
Georgia, Kentucky, Mississippi,
North Carolina, South Carolina,
Tennessee.

Regional Director, Region V
Room 758
230 South Dearborn Street
Chicago, Illinois 60604
States served: Illinois, Indiana,
Michigan, Minnesota, Ohio,
Wisconsin.

Regional Director, Region VI
Room 502 Federal Building
525 Griffin Street
Dallas, Texas 75202
States served: Arkansas,
Louisiana, New Mexico,
Oklahoma, Texas.

Regional Director, Region VII
1100 Federal Office Building
911 Walnut Street
Kansas City, Missouri 64106
States served: Iowa, Kansas,
Missouri, Nebraska.

Regional Director, Region VIII
Room 476
U.S. Custom House
721 - 19th Street
Denver, Colorado 80202
States served: Colorado,
Montana, North Dakota, South
Dakota, Utah, Wyoming.

Regional Director, Region IX
Federal Building, Room 715
71 Stevenson Street
San Francisco, California 94119
States served: Arizona,
California, Hawaii, Nevada.

Regional Director, Region X
1111 Third Avenue—Room 925
Seattle, Washington 98101-2121
States served: Alaska, Idaho,
Oregon, Washington.

STATE APPRENTICESHIP COUNCILS/AGENCIES

Arizona

Apprentice Services
Arizona Department of Economic
Security
438 West Adams Street
Phoenix, Arizona 85003

California

Division of Apprentice Standards
3950 Oyster Point Boulevard
Suite 500, C Wing
San Francisco, California 94080

Connecticut

Office of Job Training and Skill
Development
Connecticut Labor Department
200 Folly Brook Boulevard
Wethersfield, Connecticut 06109

District of Columbia

DC Apprenticeship Council
500 C. Street, N.W., Suite 241
Washington, D.C. 20001

Delaware

Apprenticeship and Training Section
Division of Employment &
Training
Delaware Department of Labor
6th Floor, State Office Building
820 North French Street
Wilmington, Delaware 19601

Florida

Bureau of Apprenticeship
  Division of Labor, Employment
  & Training
Department of Labor &
  Employment Security
1320 Executive Center Drive,
  Atkins Building
Tallahassee, Florida 32301

Hawaii

Apprenticeship Division
Department of Labor & Industrial
  Relations
830 Punch Bowl Street
Honolulu, Hawaii 96813

Kansas

Kansas State Apprenticeship Council
Department of Human Resources
401 SW Topeka Boulevard
Topeka, Kansas 66603-3182

Kentucky

Apprenticeship and Training
620 South Third Street
Louisville, Kentucky 40602

Louisiana

Louisiana Department of Labor
5360 Florida Boulevard
Baton Rouge, Louisiana

M.I.

Apprenticeship Training Division
  Guam Community College
P.O. Box 23069
Guam, M.I. 96921

Maine

Bureau of Labor Standards
  State House Station #45
Augusta, Maine 04333

Maryland

Apprenticeship & Training Council
1100 North Utah Street
Room 310
Baltimore, Maryland 21201

Massachusetts

Department of Labor & Industries
Division of Apprentice Training
Leverett Saltonstall Bldg.
100 Cambridge Street
Boston, Massachusetts 02202

Minnesota

Division of Apprenticeship
  Department of Labor & Industry
Space Center Building, 4th Floor
443 Lafayette Road
St. Paul, Minnesota 55101

Montana

Apprenticeship & Training
  Bureau of Employment, Policy
    Division
  Department of Labor & Industry
P.O. Box 1728
Helena, Montana 59620

Nevada

Nevada State Apprenticeship
  Council
505 East King St. Room 601
P.O. Box 4452
Carson City, Nevada 89710

New Hampshire

New Hampshire Apprenticeship
  Council
19 Pillsbury Street
Concord, New Hampshire 03301

New Mexico

Apprenticeship Bureau
  New Mexico Department of Labor
  501 Mountain Road, N.E.
  Albuquerque, New Mexico 12240

New York

NYS Department of Labor
  State Office Campus
  Building #12 L Room 140
  Albany, New York 12240

North Carolina

North Carolina Department of Labor
  4 West Edenton Street
  Raleigh, North Carolina 27601

Ohio

Ohio State Apprenticeship Council
  2323 West 5th Avenue, Room
  2140
  Columbus, Ohio 43216

Oregon

Apprenticeship & Training Division
  Room 405, State Office Building
  1400 South West Fifth Avenue
  Portland, Oregon 97201

Pennsylvania

Apprenticeship and Training
  1303 Labor & Industry Building
  7th and Forster St., Room 1303
  Harrisburg, Pennsylvania 17120

Puerto Rico

Incentive to the Private Sector
  Program
  P.O. Box 4452
  505 Munoz Rivera Avenue
  San Juan, Puerto Rico 00936

Rhode Island

RI State Apprenticeship Shore
  Council
  200 Elmwood Avenue
  Providence, Rhode Island 02907

Vermont

Apprenticeship and Training
  Department of Labor & Industry
  120 State Street
  Montpelier, Vermont 05602

Virgin Islands

Division of Apprenticeship &
    Training
  Department of Labor
  P.O. Box 890, Christiansted
  St. Croix, Virgin Islands 00802

Virginia

Division of Labor & Industry
  P.O. Box 12064
  Richmond, Virginia 23241

Washington

Department of Labor and Industries,
    ESAC Division
  General Administration Building
  MS HC-730
  Olympia, Washington 98504-0631

Wisconsin

Department of Industry, Labor and
    Human Relations
  Employment & Training Policy
    Division
  P.O. Box 7972
  Madison, Wisconsin 53707

GLOSSARY

Application: A computer program used for a particular kind of work, such as word processing or database management.

Artificial intelligence (AI):   A computer with AI has the ability to mimic human reasoning or sensing. Within AI, expert systems are computer systems that function close to the level of human expert knowledge. Expert systems applications include design and cost-estimating systems used by General Motors and Ford in the process of making automobiles.

ASCII: American National Standard Code for Information Interchange, a standard file format that lets different types of computers interpret information in the same way.

Byte: A basic unit of communication between computers. A byte consists of eight bits. Data passes between computers as streams of bytes.

CAD: see computer-aided design.

CADD: Computer-aided design and drafting.

CAE: Computer-aided engineering.

CAM: see Computer-aided manufacturing.

CASA/SME: Computer & Automated Systems Association, Society of Manufacturing Engineers.

CD-ROM: Compact disc-read-only memory; a compact disc on which computer data can be stored and accessed.

Chamfer: In CAD, a beveled edge.

CIM: see Computer-integrated manufacturing.

CNC: see Computer numerically-controlled.

Computer & Automated Systems/Society of Manufacturing Engineers (CASA/SME): One society of SME.

Computer-aided design (CAD): Using the computer to create, modify, or evaluate product design. A CAD program often combines design techniques and manufacturing principles. In architecture, CAD includes drawing, drafting, and modeling, as well as the management of information.

Computer-aided manufacturing (CAM): Using the computer to plan, control, and operate the production of a product.

Computer-integrated manufacturing (CIM): (pronounced "sim") Using a computer to coordinate activities from market forecasting, sales, and engineering through production and distribution.

Computer numerically controlled (CNC): Machine tools or machines controlled by a computer. Often, CNC machines are equipped with a screen and keyboard for writing and editing numerically controlled programs at the machine.

Cursor: The small light on the monitor that shows you where you are when you're working on the computer.

Database: A collection of organized information. In CAD/CAM, the geometry of parts, described as mathematical coordinates. Computers can transmit, process, and change the data. They can compile it, and handle all kinds of information about the part. In CAD/CAM, the database is a common filing system.

Database management system: A system that stores and retrieves information in a database. A *relational* database management system lets you organize your data according to subject, and store information about how different subjects are related. Because the computer "knows" how the information in data files are related, you can easily organize and analyze data from different tables stored in the database.

Design: The entire process of conceptualizing and documenting a project, including all stages of drawing.

Desktop publishing: Computer software systems that combine word processing and graphics with the ability to lay out and print pages.

Digital: A signal encoded as a series of discrete numbers.

Digitize: The process by which the coordinates of a point are stored in the computer.

Drafting: Drawing a preliminary sketch or plan.

DXF (Drawing Interchange Format) files: A proprietary file translation format developed by Autodesk; the de facto standard in CAD. DXF files let you exchange drawings between various CAD programs.

Electronic Data Interexchange (EDI): Sending data electronically between terminals . . . an important strategic tool for effective, efficient business operations.

Electronic mail: Also known as E-mail, in which messages are sent electronically from one computer to another.

Ergonomics: The human factor involved in work.

Ethernet: A widely installed version of a standard used in networking. Ethernet is often used in computer rooms and in terminal-to-mainframe links in offices.

Expert systems: Computer programs that separate the "knowledge base" from information about the current problem ("input data") and methods ("inferences") for applying the knowledge to the problem. Expert systems are different from conventional computer programs, in which knowledge is intertwined with methods for using the knowledge.

Fileserver: The central storage location on a network that "keeps" applications and data files. Files can be retrieved from the fileserver, worked on at a workstation or individual PC, and then saved to the fileserver. A local area network (LAN) generally has a single, central fileserver. Some LANs are configured with distributed servers, which are many fileservers scattered among workstations.

Fillet: An arc that merges two intersecting lines.

Finite element analysis: A way of checking a CAD design through special software that analyzes factors such as stress, vibration, heat transfer, and kinematics. For instance, FEA software can determine the interaction of parts in an assembly to estimate stress distribution or heat transfer. This information is useful for modifying the shape of a component.

Flexible manufacturing cell: Usually, a system of several machine tools, sometimes served by a robot, for producing a family of related parts, often in small batches.

Flexible manufacturing system: An integrated system of automated machines, equipment, and work-and-tool transport apparatus that operates under computer control.

GIS: Geographic information systems.

Group technology: In manufacturing, looking at product parts, identifying common points, and then processing those various parts that have common features together or in sequence.

GUI: Graphical user interface. Symbols that identify keyboard functions.

Hardware: The "nuts and bolts" of a computer system.

Icon: A graphical representation of various elements.

Initial Graphics Exchange Specification (IGES): A file translation format that's understood by other CAD systems. Designers and drafters can exchange data easily, whether or not they use the same CAD system. IGES is recognized by the National Bureau of Standards as a system for transferring graphic information between computer programs.

Institute of Industrial Engineers (IIE): A professional association.

Integrated modeling: Three-dimensional modeling that includes the ability to draft, dimension, and plot two-dimensional drawings within a three-dimensional context.

Laptops: Generally in the 10–25 pound range, these are computers that can be transported. Some have non-battery-operated systems.

Layer: A means of grouping similar drawing elements so that they may be manipulated together.

Local area network (LAN):   Network in which several computers are tied together, using telecommunications technology. Large LANs are usually server-based networks, which keep program and data files together on a central hard disk. Most smaller sub-LANs are networks in which each personal computer has its own set of files that only one user can retrieve at any time. LANs make it possible for numbers of users with individual personal computers to share expensive peripherals, such as large hard disks and laser printers. At the same time, LANs provide efficiency, database integrity, and security.

Machine vision: A system in which a TV camera/computer produces a matrix of digitized dots ("pixels") for information about intensity and range. The computer analyzes pixels for patterns or edge detection, usually by recalculating large matrices of numbers rapidly and by searching through the computer's huge "dictionary" of possible objects. Machine vision is concerned with inspection, recognition, and measurement.

Manufacturing Automation Protocol (MAP):   An electronic link developed by General Motors and vendors that joins together computers, terminals, numerically controlled devices and robotics, using a common protocol that lets machines from different vendors "talk" to each other.

Manufacturing execution system: The collection of systems that are needed to manage, monitor, and control all production and production-related activities at the facility level where the execution takes place. These systems track all the elements of manufacturing—equipment, labor, machines, and the environment—and integrate them through a relational database.

Modem: A device that translates digital signals from a computer to analog signals that can be transmitted over telephone lines. When the signals reach the receiving computer, another modem translates them back to digital signals. This conversion process lets computers send data to each other. The process is called MOdulation-DEModulation.

Mouse: A hand-operated graphic input device. Moving the mouse makes the cursor move in a corresponding direction, and at a corresponding rate. A mouse does not digitize. Instead, it remembers points incrementally. All program locations are given in terms of distance and direction from the immediately preceding point.

MS-DOS: The most widely used operating system for personal computers.

Multimedia: Broadly defined, a group of technologies that combine full-motion video, animation, still pictures, voice, music, graphics and text into a fully integrated, interactive system. Its potential users include training, education, publishing, entertainment, voice/video mail, teleconferencing, public information, and document imaging and archival systems (potentially useful in CAD/CAM applications). Industry sources project a $13 billion multimedia market by 1995.

Network: A way in which signals or data can be shared by computers. Resources are linked together so information can be sent where it is needed. A local area network (LAN) is one type of network that uses cables, lines, and software to connect various computer devices to send and receive data.

Non-uniform rational B-splines (NURBS): Two-dimensional analogs of spline curves, used to design free-form surfaces that can't be described by planes, cylinders, and conic sections.

Notebooks: Portable computers that weigh under 10 pounds, with two or more hours of battery life and a full-size keyboard.

Numerical control (NC):   Controlling processes automatically by interpreting data that have been prerecorded in symbolic form, usually on tapes or computer programs.

Open architecture: A philosophy of software design which allows users of a program to customize the software to fit specific requirements—no matter what they may be.

OSI: Open Systems Interconnect. An architecture for computer networks, and a family of standards that permits data communication and data processing among diverse technologies. OSI-based standards anticipate the development of particular applications or products. They provide a reference model that defines and categorizes seven layers of functions that need to be performed in the protocols and services at each level. OSI-based standards are international in scope, and are being developed in international standard-setting bodies.

Personal computer: Also called a PC, this is a self-contained computer with its own monitor, data entry unit, and processing unit. A PC is a single-user, general application computer based on a single microprocessor chip with a resident operating system and local programming capability.

Pixel: A small cell, part of a picture area. Each pixel is a picture element or one phosphor or dot on the screen. It is illuminated by an electron gun that sweeps from left to right or from top to bottom on the screen. The resolution of a monitor is judged by the number of pixels on the screen. In simple systems, each cell contains either color or no color. In more complex systems, each cell contains one of a range of colors and shades. Used in machine vision.

Programmable automation: Automation that performs a variety of tasks by using computer and communications technology. Generally, programmable automation is divided into CAD, CAM, and computer-aided techniques for management, especially management information systems and computer-aided planning.

Rapid prototyping and manufacturing (RP&M):   A new technology capable of generating physical objects directly from a graphical computer base. CAD is used to design the original prototype, and to correct errors in the part after it's been built. Leading aerospace, automotive, component, and medical device manufacturing corporations have begun to use RP&M.

Rasterizing: A process by which the software translates vector graphics into a matrix of dots.

Rendering: In architecture, a representation of a building or object, done in perspective. In CAD, often, a shaded, colored drawing that's shown to clients as part of a presentation.

RIA: Robotic Industries Association, the trade organization for robot users and manufacturers, robot equipment suppliers, research institutes, consultants, systems suppliers, educational institutions, and other companies interested in developing and using robot technology.

RI/SME: Robotics International/Society of Manufacturing Engineers, one of SME's societies.

Robot: A reprogrammable, multifunctional manipulator designed to move material, parts, tools, or specialized devices through variable programmed motions for the performance of a variety of tasks. (RIA definition: the Japanese define "robot" more broadly.)

RS-232: An interconnect standard between computer hardware and peripherals, such as a printer or modem. Under this standard, the computer sends single bits of information to the printer, one after the other.

Simulation: A computer process by which robots and other machine tools can be "made" to perform on a computer screen through pictorial representation. Users can see what the machines will do and how they will do it. Simulation—which can be described as the "what ifs?"—is accomplished through high-tech computer software.

Society of Manufacturing Engineers (SME):A major professional association; one of the largest and most influential associations concerned with CAD/CAM.

Software: The programs that make the computers do the tasks you want them to.

Solid modeling: The ability—on-screen—to create a CAD drawing that lets you observe the actual spatial relationship of components within that drawing. Solid modeling CAD systems generate an unambiguous description of the geometry being modeled.

Standard Industrial Classification (SIC) codes: The U.S. government's system used for gathering data on economic activity. SIC codes divide this activity into nine major categories (i.e., manufacturing). These categories are divided into major groups, which have 2-digit codes; then, into industry groups, which have 3-digit codes; then, into industries, which have 4-digit codes. For instance, aircraft engines and engine parts are SIC 3724.

StereoLithography (SL):   The first of the rapid prototyping systems. SL involves a unique combination of polymer chemistry, laser physics, optics, material science, viscous fluid dynamics, computer science, and electrical and mechanical engineering.

*.STL: A file format that's virtually an industry standard for input to rapid prototyping systems.

Structured Query Language (SQL):   A computer statement that queries, updates, or manages a relational database. See Database management system.

SWE: Society of Women Engineers.

Technical Office Protocol (TOP):   Developed by Boeing, TOP concentrates on technical and office protocol, or the electronic link between engineering and office functions.

Turnkey: An arrangement in which the vendor supplies the entire system, hardware and software. Usually, with a turnkey system, training and service are also supplied by the same vendor.

UNIX: A proprietary operating system created by AT&T that is a multiuser/multitasking system.

VAX: A proprietary mainframe computer from Digital Equipment Corporation (DEC).

Vector: A mathematical value that represents direction and distance. Vectors are used in storage and display of CAD graphics.

Very High Speed Integrated Circuit Project: A Department of Defense project that created the VHSIC hardware description language, *VDHL.* This sophisticated, state-of-the-art hardware design language (which has become an Institute of Electrical and Electronic Engineering standard) is widely used in the computer-assisted engineering industry. *Computer Aided Design Report,* a trade newsletter, calls VHDL the international standard for top-down design of digital electronics.

Virtual Reality: The ability to interact with data in a way that enables users to "enter" and navigate through a computer-generated 3D environment and change their viewpoint and interact with objects created within that environment.

Window: A rectangular area on a computer screen in which a user views an application or a document.

Windows: A Software developed by Microsoft that provides a sophisticated graphical environment . . . a graphical user interface (GUI) that works with MS-DOS. Under Windows, a PC user can run more than one application at a time and transfer information between applications.

Windows applications: Any application that was designed especially for Windows and will not run without Windows. All Windows applications follow the same conventions for arrangement of menus, style of dialog boxes, and use of the keyboard and mouse.

Windows NT (New Technology): A 32-bit, multitasking operating system developed by Microsoft that's more technically advanced than earlier operating systems such as MS-DOS. It's expected to stimulate product development and competition in the CAD/CAM/CAE industry. Windows NT and other 32-bit systems take advantage of the graphic and networking capabilities of 32-bit PCs to decrease the technological gap between PCs and larger systems, such as workstations and mainframes. In 1993, over 30,000 developers were creating Windows NT applications, with extensive support for Windows NT coming from the CAD/CAM community.

Wireframe CAD system: A system that creates an image by using groups of lines and polygons to form transparent representations of objects. The edges or outlines of objects are displayed as lines. Usually all lines are displayed, unless hidden lines are removed.

Workstation: Most often, a single-user computer system with advanced graphics capabilities that compete in price and performance with the fastest personal computers at the low end and mini-supercomputers at the high end. Some models of workstations are multiuser servers in networked environments. Originally used in scientific and engineering applications, workstations are also beginning to be used for electronic publishing, business graphics, financial services, mapping, and office automation.

WYSIWYG: Pronounced "wissy-wig," the acronym stands for "what you see is what you get." In other words, what's on the computer screen is what gets printed.